Dave & Claudia Arp

A
JANET
THOMA
BOOK

THOMAS NELSON PUBLISHERS
Nashville

Published in Nashville, Tennessee, by Thomas Nelson, Inc., Publishers, and distributed in Canada by Word Communications, Ltd., Richmond, British Columbia, and in the United Kingdom by Word (UK), Ltd., Milton Keynes, England.

Printed in the United States of America

This book is a resource for marriage enrichment, not a substitute for needed professional counselling. If some of the exercises contained in this book raise issues for you or your spouse that cannot be easily resolved, we urge you to seek professional help.

The names of the individuals in the stories within have been changed to protect their privacy.

ISBN: 0-7852-8250-0

Dedication

We would like to dedicate this book to all of our new friends who participated in the July 1993 United Marriage Encounter International Celebration at Mount Sequoyah Conference Center, in Fayetteville, Arkansas, where we were your keynote speaker couple. You loved us and treated us as one of your own, so it is to you we dedicate this fun getaway. We hope you will personally "enjoy" it. May God richly bless your ministry and outreach to couples!

John & Blanche Ahrens
Dick & Sonnie Andersen
Philip & Marlene Bauman
Nick & Judy Becker
Roger & Kathy Becker
John & Kay Berry
Mike & Terry Bishop
Chuck & Glee Bos
Dave & Kathy Braden
Jim & Marlene Campbell
Phil & Claudia Cargill
Fred & Nancy Carter
Dave & Diann Conquest
Bob & Diane Dean
Mark & Susan DeVincentis
Geoff & Linda Dunaway
Joe & Lee Freese
Larry & Pat Gainer
Chuck & Darlene Gillette
Randy & Dale Ann Goslin
Rick & Nancy Grace
Gary & Corrin Hentzel
Gene & Cheryl Higgs
Dave & Roma Ingram
Ron & Connie Johnson
Randy & Sue Kaiser

Bruce & Marilyn Kelly
Joe & Polly Klimson
Dennis & Nancy Kneip
Harry & Char Knutsen
Gary & Jodie Layne
Ray & Ruth Mahlo
Duane & Bonnie Marburger
Kenneth & Ginny Maxwell
David & Rebecca McDanel
Ken & Shirley McDaniel
George & Diane McIlrath
Mark & Cindy Meinert
Robert & Lorraine Meyer
Kevin & Norma Moore
Ron & Linda Moore
Bob & Norma Morrison
Bill & Phyllis Nelson
Ben & Barb Newcomb
Bob & Bonnie Nicolai
Roy & Marilyn Nutter
Brad & Diana Palmer
Tim & Lee Pretz
Dal & Rusty Queck
Bob & Anita Reed
Ron & Margie Rees
John & Eula Rehberg

John & Laurie Riggs
Frederick & Joyce Robinson
Mike & Jo Anne Ruby
Ron & Sandi Sacco
Glenn & Patti Scheer
John & Susan Shaddle
Seward & Sally Shaddock
John & Karen Sitler
Dave & Jeanie Stanley
Steve & Julie Stroebele
Al & Donna Stubbs
Dean & Milly Taylor
Don & Nancy Jo Taylor
David & Ruth Thorne
Lowell & Norma Titus
John & Merelyn Voss
Joel & Margret Walker
Lynn & Carol Walter
Gregg & Zelda Walther
Keith & Karen Waterman
Jerry & Carol Webb
Loren & Linda Wiese
Harley & Ruthanne Woodhouse
Don & Barb Zahrobsky

Contents

Acknowledgments

Any attempt to list all those who gave us input on this book would be incomplete. However, we especially want to acknowledge and express our appreciation to the following:

Thanks to all the couples across the United States including our sons and daughters-in-law who spent a weekend testing this resource. Your input was invaluable!

Thanks to Vera Mace and her late husband David R. Mace, who have been wonderful mentors, friends, and encouragers to us, and to the Association for Couples in Marriage Enrichment (A.C.M.E.) founded by the Maces.

Thanks to United Marriage Encounter (U.M.E.) and *Marriage Partnership* magazine for your input.

Thanks to all the couples everywhere who have worked at having a growing healthy marriage. Since marriage exercises are like folklore (we may never know the original source), thanks to everyone who contributed to our Mini Marriage Builders—even those we don't know!

Thanks to our pastor, John Wood, for his biblical wisdom.

Our special thanks to Robert Zaloba for challenging us with the concept of this book. And finally to Janet Thoma, Susan Salmon Trotman, Laurie Clark, and the in-house staff at Thomas Nelson, thank you for helping us pull this book together and make it a reality!

PART ONE

BEFORE THE GETAWAY

"Our weekend was terrific! We spent a lot of time walking and talking. We even rented mopeds for Saturday afternoon—something we literally haven't done for years! It was a great activity for the 'Fun and Fresh Air' time."

Married eleven years, two children

"Initially this getaway interested me because we could tailor it to us, and it didn't require a lot of preparation and writing. (I do so much of that at work!) Yet it sparked some serious discussions. It was more fun than I expected. My favorite part of the weekend was watching an old movie and eating snacks while we were snuggled under the covers. My husband hates crumbs in the bed, so we never get to do that at home!"

Married two years

"On our weekend we even tackled a biggie we needed to talk about— finances! The Mini Marriage Builders helped us deal with this and other problem areas in a nonthreatening way. We're still friends and have a plan for debt reduction: baking some of our credit cards!"

Married twenty-three years, three children

"We loved holding hands, listening to music, and talking about our memories. We even wrote them down to save for posterity. We definitely plan to do another weekend and will use the Mini Marriage Builders in our Marriage Encounter small groups."

Married thirty years, two grown children

Chapter One

Saying "Yes" to Your Marriage

Comments like those on the previous page from couples who recently participated in their first do-it-yourself *Ultimate Marriage Builder* getaway weekend excite us. Over the years, as we have led our Marriage Alive Workshops, we've felt the frustration and disappointment of those who can't seem to motivate their mates to attend a marriage enrichment or marriage encounter weekend.

It doesn't necessarily mean these mates aren't interested in improving their marriages—but with jobs, kids, church, school, community service, and the ten other things they are involved in, there's no time or energy left over for their spouses. Or maybe there are some problems, and they are afraid to look honestly at their relationships, especially in a group.

Recently, as we were speaking at a "Brown Bag with the Authors" luncheon on our book, *The Marriage Track*, one husband commented, "Wild horses wouldn't get my wife, Ethel, to a marriage conference of any description. I know better than to try!"

One wife aired her frustration: "Whenever I talk to Harry about working on our marriage, all I hear is, 'Don't fix it if it ain't broke!' Isn't there some way we can re-ignite that ole spark?"

Our answer? Emphatically, "Yes!" For Harry, Ethel, their spouses, and all who would like a marriage booster, there is a simple way to infuse your relationship with fun, romance, and intimacy. Like the couples at the beginning of this chapter, you can experience your own *Ultimate Marriage Builder* getaway weekend!

GETAWAY FOR TWO

Interested? Then this book is just for you. More than a getaway weekend, the *ULTIMATE MARRIAGE BUILDER*, a do-it-yourself encounter weekend for you and your mate, provides you with exercises and activities to better understand each other, improve your communication, deal with real issues, and reaffirm your commitment to one another. This weekend getaway can result in greater intimacy, and can be the basis for future marital growth.

Ultimate marriages don't just happen, but many people think they do! One problem in our complicated world is that we simply have not been trained how to build positive relationships. We can send men to the moon, travel faster than the speed of sound, fax information halfway across the world in a matter of seconds, and access think tanks with our computers, but we lack the interpersonal competence needed to build loving relationships. Why?

The Marital Taboo

Marriage specialists Dr.'s David and Vera Mace have an answer. They call it the "Marital Taboo." You just don't talk about your marriage; therefore, many live in isolation from others and assume:

1. No special knowledge and skills are required to make a marriage work.

2. Most marriages are okay and free from problems. (If you believe this then you may be living with deep disappointment or disillusionment.)

3. There is a common belief that conflict is destructive and to be avoided, so you tend to suppress anger and negative feelings. Instead of resolving anything the walls just get higher.[1]

The concept of "marital growth" doesn't really fit into our culture. Think about it. You get married, and then you are supposed to "settle down." Doesn't that sound boring?

If your marriage could do with a little stirring up, and if you're willing to take the risk and really want to slow down enough to create your own environment for growth and change, then plan your own getaway just for two!

We will be your guide and will help you choose the topics you want to talk about. You can even tackle a biggie if you both want to, or you can keep it light. It's up to you. You'll have the opportunity to reaffirm your commitment to each other and look at ways you want to grow together.

Our Three "S's"

To make the weekend work for you, you will want to include our three S's:

1. You need *seclusion*—to get away from the paralyzing pressures of the daily routine. We suggest a full forty-eight hours away, but if you can only pull off one over-night, go for it.

2. You need a *stimulus*—We'll provide that! We'll help you appreciate the positive things about your relationship and guide you in looking at what you want to change.

3. The last "S" that you need is "*some fun.*" We tried to think of a synonym for fun that began with an "S" and couldn't until a friend suggested "Sex!" So just to let you know up front, your getaway will include romance.

The only thing else needed is your commitment. So if you want to revitalize your relationship with fun, romance, and intimacy, go ahead, say "Yes" to your marriage! Plan your *Ultimate Marriage Builder Getaway*.

Chapter Two

Setting the Stage

When we think about planning a getaway, one of our most favorite places to go is in the mountains near Sisters, Oregon. It meets the three "S" requirement. It's secluded—you have to know the code just to get onto the property. It's stimulating. Inspiration abounds. The head of the Metolius River snakes through green pastures with cows grazing and families of ducks strutting all around. In the background, you can see llamas and the beautiful snow-capped mountains. The last "S"— some fun—we provide!

We're always looking for some way to get back to Sisters. So on the front end of a recent trip out west to record radio programs for The Family Workshop, it seemed logical to piggyback a visit to the Oregon mountains. Not smart! We quickly discovered that right after recording 68 two-minute spots (all with high energy and enthusiasm about marriage and family life) was not the ideal time for a marriage getaway.

Tired, emotionally exhausted, and not in the best of health, we arrived at our favorite romantic spot. Romantic? You've got to be kidding! Of the three "S's," all we experienced was seclusion—from each other. Dave had bronchitis and couldn't lie down without having a cough attack, so for the whole night he slept on the couch in the living room! Definitely not an *Ultimate Marriage Builder.*

Learn from us. Don't plan your getaway when you know you are going to be exhausted and under stress! Wise planning can maximize your *Ultimate Marriage Builder* weekend experience. Just follow our advice for what you need to do before your getaway.

PREPARE FOR YOUR GETAWAY

Before your getaway, you need to choose a date and location; make preparations for the kids, the pets, the job, _____ (fill in the blank), and talk about your expectations for your weekend. You don't have to do any homework ahead of time for the actual getaway. Just follow the suggestions in this chapter and you'll be ready for fun, romance, and intimacy.

It's great to plan your getaway together, but if one of you has more time and/or interest, take the initiative and do the research. Your tired, overworked mate will thank you! Here's what one wife who had been married for two years told us: "I surprised Michael with the weekend. He couldn't believe I was doing anything like this because he's usually the instigator of this sort of thing. He kept saying all weekend, 'I can't believe you did this!'"

Collect brochures of places to go such as:

- bed and breakfasts
- beach condos
- mountain cabins
- campgrounds

If finances are tight, consider trading houses with friends (they stay in your house with your children *and* theirs! Later you can return the favor). Jim and Janice, who both travel in their jobs, told us they like to just stay at home and not answer the phone. "It's a real treat," Janice said, "to plan a getaway at home and stay put with our own Jacuzzi, music system, and comfortable bed!" However, if you follow Jim and Janice's example, you must use willpower and resist doing any little jobs you see around the house that need doing. Just pretend the housekeeping service will come in on Monday morning. This also includes a ban on any take-home work from the office!

Check with travel agencies for any special deals they may have. Some airlines offer two-for-one tickets. If you fly often, frequent flyer points are a great source of free tickets. Travel clubs offer free maps and routing services. Once you have finished your research, you're ready to make firm plans for your getaway.

Pick Your Time and Place

Together choose a date and location for your getaway. Make reservations and find the bucks you need in your budget. Also you may want to choose an alternate date just in case someone gets sick or something unforeseeable happens.

If you have the need, arrange for child care. To ensure your peace of mind, consider writing a medical permission form that enables your child care provider to seek treatment in a medical emergency. It should also give your child care provider information on how to reach you in the unlikely event of an emergency. Now to the fun part of planning—the *getaway box!*

The Getaway Box

We suggest that you actually designate a *getaway box*. (If you're the creative type, you could stencil it with hearts or decorate it in your own unique style.) One couple, married twelve years with two children, told us, "Our getaway box was a big hit and now is an excellent ongoing reminder. We keep it out and are collecting things for our next getaway!"

What goes in the getaway box? Some of the items that might go in your box are:

• Candles and candle holders. (Scented candles are nice, don't forget matches!)
• Music cassettes with a cassette player (or CDs). See if you can find *your song* from years gone by. Our song is from the movie, "A Summer Place." That's the movie we saw on our first date. Just recently we saw one survey that rated it one of the most romantic movies ever. We agree!

- Your favorite snacks and drinks. (You may want to include two crystal glasses or china cups and saucers—just be sure to pack them well!)

- Shop for new lingerie or bathrobes. (We have two white terry cloth bathrobes that we save for our away times. They are just plain robes, but are special because we don't wear them at home—only when we are away.)

- Bath accessories, such as bubble bath, baby oil, and sweet smelling things. (This may be a great time to try out a new perfume or aftershave lotion.)

- Add whatever you know your mate would really enjoy having along like the *Wall Street Journal*—unless this would put your workaholic mate into a business mode. (If this happens, use the paper the first evening to start the fire!) One friend shared that she would definitely add books for her husband who is the real intellectual type and wouldn't even look at a book that weighed less than five pounds! Remember you don't have to spend every waking moment of your getaway together, so bring things you might enjoy doing alone.

- Golf clubs, tennis racquets, games, swimsuits, hiking boots. Think about the things you really enjoy doing but seldom get to do at home.

- Wedding album or early pictures of the two of you.

- Bible, favorite daily devotional guide, prayer notebook.

- Loose-leaf notebooks, pens, and blank paper will be helpful. You may also want to bring a hole punch and scissors for removing pages from this guide that you'll want to transfer to your own personal notebook. One couple suggests decorating the front (they called it a Lover's Cover) of your *weekend getaway notebook* with hearts or whatever appeals to you.

- A small box or container for the exercise on Friday night.
- As unromantic as it may sound, take your planning calendars. You just might end up scheduling more romantic times together for the future!
- Why not bring one little surprise gift to give your mate sometime during the weekend? It doesn't have to be expensive, but please, no toasters, can openers, weed eaters, dust busters, or anything that can be plugged into an outlet!

What to Leave at Home:

- Any kind of work or correspondence.
- Computers and printers. (We know one couple who took both! Us!)
- Beeper, fax, or cellular phone.
- Children (pets are optional).
- Definitely not a good weekend for a double date!
- For us, we try to leave all manuscripts at home!

PLAN YOUR WEEKEND AGENDA

Now that you've made your physical arrangements and have your getaway box all ready to go, find a time to talk about your expectations and what you are going to do on your weekend. This will set the tone for your time away, so consider going someplace where you can be alone and won't be interrupted, like out to eat dinner or dessert, or even to the park for a picnic.

The main purpose of this time is to talk about your expectations and plan the agenda for the weekend. One wife told us to tell people not to skip this part. She said, "We started learning about one another from the moment we started talking about our expectations. This was a surprise! It really helped our weekend go smoothly."

A WORD TO THE WISE: Don't overplan! This getaway is not intended to be *work*. Its purpose is to revitalize your relationship.

Do not try to do everything in this book in one weekend. There are lots of options to choose from. But this is not a course you have to finish. Set your own pace—one that is comfortable for you.

Marriage is a marathon, not a sprint. The *Ultimate Marriage Builder* just-for-two encounter weekend is more than a one-time experience. There are enough resources here for a number of getaways. So remember, if you don't get through your chosen agenda, don't worry about it.

If you relax, have fun, and make some progress, your marriage getaway will be successful.

Your Getaway Options

Let us whet your appetite and tell you some of your options for your getaway. Think about this book as you would a menu at your favorite restaurant where, perhaps, you even know the chef. Prominent on the menu would be the chef's selections, the dishes he personally recommends.

As your weekend chef, we have selected five exercises that cover the essential areas of marital growth. If this is your first *Ultimate Marriage Builder* getaway weekend, we suggest you build your weekend around these. Let us preview them with you.

Friday Evening has already been planned for you. (It's like the complimentary hors d'oeuvres you get at fine restaurants.) We know you will probably be tired, so we've planned a light, relaxing evening. The topic is "Rekindling the Spark." You'll have the opportunity to talk about some of your favorite memories. Then we offer a fun exercise to top off your evening.

Saturday Morning we suggest you start your day with "Vive la Différence." This *Ultimate Marriage Builder* exercise will give you a chance to look at the ways you are alike and the ways you are different and how you complement one another.

Saturday Afternoon the "Fun and Fresh Air" exercise will help you fine-tune your communication and learn some new things about each other. There will be plenty of free time for whatever you want to do, from napping to taking a long walk in the woods.

Saturday Evening is time for dessert. We highly recommend "Romancing Your Mate."

Sunday you will have the opportunity to plan for the future. This exercise is called "Room to Grow."

Marriage à la Carte

We have also provided "à la carte" exercises for you to choose from, which we call *Mini Marriage Builders*. Each is a short, practical exercise that will be a catalyst to a meaningful conversation. The Mini Marriage Builders deal with a large range of topics. Some are light—like "The Encouragement Exercise" and "Rut Busters"—and others deal with heavier subjects, such as issues in your marriage that you both want to address. You might choose the "Learning to Negotiate" exercise. If you have a problem controlling your temper, or if you have some specific issues to work through, "Learning to Process Anger" may be helpful.

Do you have tension in your marriage because you want everything to be perfect? That may be a noble goal, but "Taming Perfection" will help you find balance. "The Bible on Sex" exercise may help you overcome inhibitions and "Choosing Chores" will help you settle whose job it really is to take out the garbage!

At any point during the weekend you can choose what you want to talk about. It's your call. To supplement your weekend we have over fifty Mini Marriage Builder exercises—obviously more than can be completed in one weekend. (See chapter 8.) Pick and choose. It's totally up to you.

Couples who have experienced our weekend getaway seem to love the Mini Marriage Builders. One couple, married seven years with two children, commented, "The Mini Marriage Builders were so helpful to us in a non-threatening way. We could decide what we would talk about as well as what we didn't want to discuss on our weekend."

Another couple married five years with a blended family of six children said, "We were able to talk about our budget without getting angry with each other. We even set up a special fund for another getaway."

Great Expectations

There may already be some things you know you want to talk about during your getaway, or things you would like to do. We each come with expectations, and it helps us to talk about them beforehand. A game we like to play from time to time, and especially when we are getting ready for a getaway, is the game, "I'm looking forward to." Here's how you can play:

Separately, make a list of things you are looking forward to for the weekend. For instance, Dave usually looks forward to sleeping late and having no schedule. Claudia hopes to get in a long walk together and have some time for reading that novel she has carried on our last two trips.

We suggest you each make your list separately and then share your lists with each other.

I'm looking forward to:

_____

_____

_____

_____

Ask, "Are our expectations realistic?" Claudia's list is usually over-crowded while Dave may have only a few things on his. Together we balance each other and start our encounter with more realistic expectations.

SETTING GETAWAY GUIDELINES

The next step is to set your own getaway guidelines. Here are some of the guidelines we have used that worked for us.

1. We agree to stay positive.
2. We will assume the best.
3. Our goal is to build our relationship and have fun.
4. We will not talk about our children or work unless it relates to a specific topic we are talking about.
5. We will not bring along any work to do.

We have even gone so far as to sign a pre-getaway agreement. Anticipation grows as we know ahead of time some of the things we want to talk about. Our pre-getaway agreement from one of our getaway weekends is on page 19.

Now it's your turn. Complete this chapter by writing out your own pre-getaway agreement. Don't forget to sign it. What happens if you break your agreement? It will simply help you refocus. As this wife discovered, "I broke the *No conversations about work* agreement three times before sundown on Saturday!" (That was probably pretty good for her!)

For Our Getaway, We Agree To:

"We agree to leave work, worries, and other cares at home, realizing they won't go away and will patiently wait for our return. Claudia will compromise and let Dave take the notebook computer along, but with the following restrictions: Dave will not play with any new programs or Managing Your Money (unless financial planning is one of our chosen Mini Marriage Builders). For this weekend, we choose to leave the TV, VCR, and radio unplugged. Reluctantly, Claudia agrees to have someone else check our voice mail and to resist calling to get it herself. For forty-eight hours we will concentrate on each other and on our marriage relationship. Other goals for the weekend include discussing retirement planning and how to focus and slow down a bit, as well as planning a fun just-for-two vacation for this next year."

Signed: _____

_____

For Our Getaway, We Agree To:

_____
_____
_____
_____
_____
_____
_____
_____
_____
_____
_____
_____
_____
_____
_____
_____
_____
_____
_____
_____

Signed: _____

_____

Now get ready for a fun weekend away. Along with our
Marriage Encounter friends we emphatically say,
"Enjoy, enjoy, enjoy!"

PART TWO

THE
GETAWAY

Dear Friends,

Welcome to your *Ultimate Marriage Builder* weekend. We're glad you're taking the time to grow together. We hope you will relax and enjoy focusing on your marriage relationship.

You will have the opportunity to see your marriage more clearly, get to know yourself and your mate better, pay attention to each other, and laugh and affirm each other.

So come escape from the daily cares and routines. Our prayer for you is that this investment of time you have chosen to make this weekend will reap great dividends as you grow together in your marriage relationship!

Best wishes for a great getaway,

Dave & Claudia

Chapter Three

FRIDAY EVENING

Rekindling the Spark

Congratulations! You did it! You are here! Welcome to your *Ultimate Marriage Builder* getaway. We suggest you take a few minutes to unpack and settle in.

The hardest work is over and that was just getting here. If by chance you brought along any cares, worries, or concerns we'll give you a moment to let them out the door. For this weekend we only want you to think about each other. You don't even have to think about what you need to do next. So kick off your shoes, get comfortable, and when you're ready to begin, we'll be here just waiting to guide you along the way.

LAUNCHING YOUR ADVENTURE

Why are people amazed when we tell them we've been married over thirty years? We often hear, "Congratulations, that's a record in today's world." Others say things like, "How do you keep the spark alive? You both seem to really enjoy each other: what's your secret?"

"Part of our secret," we answer, "is to rekindle that ole spark by remembering when the fires of love and romance were first lit!" You can do the same. Maybe you don't feel as romantic and as close to your partner as you did before marriage. You're not sure who moved or how it happened, but you want to start moving back closer together. To help you do just that, think back to your pre-marriage days—all the way back to when you first met each other. Do you remember the first time you saw each other? The first time you were really impressed with that other person?

First Memories

The first time we saw each other, we didn't actually meet, but we did have an *encounter* of sorts. Claudia was thirteen years old and Dave—a mischievous fifteen-year-old—threw her in the swimming pool with her clothes on. While Claudia outwardly pretended to be angry, deep down inside she thought Dave was really cute; at least he had noticed her! Dave says he vaguely remembers throwing her in the pool, but doesn't really remember that much about it.

The first time he really remembers Claudia was their first date. We actually met on a blind date set up by a mutual friend of the family. Claudia even remembers what we wore. She had on a red gingham dress and Dave a dark olive green corduroy sports coat. Dave's strongest first impression of Claudia was actually after we had several dates. He was working on a bridge construction job and Claudia dropped by. "I remember her being so perky and cute, vivacious and fun, and I could tell she really liked me. For a laid-back guy," Dave adds, "remembering that much is pretty good. I also remember the car she was in. It was a two-tone Pontiac."

Claudia says she doesn't even remember her family ever owning a car like that, but she remembers how tan, handsome, and muscular Dave was that summer from working on the bridge.

As we share our memories with you, we want to facilitate your sharing your memories with each other. One couple told us they enjoyed reading straight through the next several pages, and then over dinner, they talked through their own memories. "That way," Kathy said, "we didn't keep getting interrupted by the Arps." If you like this approach, on pages 41–42 you'll find a page of memory pegs. You can tear those pages out and take them with you on your own stroll down memory lane.

Another couple preferred to follow our lead and after each question, talked about their own personal memories. Some couples preferred to just talk while others said, "Write it down, even if it's just jotting down ideas later."

Writing can be good if you need some time to reflect or if it's been a few years since you've thought about these things. Also, if one of you is a more aggressive talker or is generally more verbal than the other, be sure to give the quieter mate equal time—time to formulate thoughts—and try not to interrupt! Here are two other options: you can individually jot down your memories on a separate piece of paper before you talk about them, or you can take notes as you talk. Do what works for you. One wife said, "Mike is not a big writer/reader, but he loves to talk. So for us it worked best just to talk."

The
Getaway
___

Now it's your turn to think about your own memories and when you first met. What were some of your first impressions?

First Date

Now think about your first date. Where did you go? How did you feel? As we already indicated, we really didn't know each other before our first date. However, Dave was curious and tenacious. He kept calling Claudia, but she was always busy or out of town. Finally, the fourth time he called, we connected. We went to church where Claudia spoke to the youth group. Then we went to a drive-in movie. Dave remembers it as a pleasant time but had no great expectations. Claudia was a little more excited and nervous. (How would you like to give a talk in front of a blind date—especially a good-looking blind date?) While neither of us remembers it being exactly "an enchanted evening," we did have fun being with each other, and it led to more dates in the coming weeks.

What are the things you remember from your first date?

First Kiss

Dave can't even remember it—guess he didn't hear bells. Claudia does remember it, but remembers that Dave wasn't that good of a kisser. "He got better," she adds. Amazingly, the more romantic memory was the first time we held hands. We know, that really dates us. But we're not unique; listen to another couple's memories: "It was fun to remember our first touch. The first time we touched hands was more memorable for both of us than our first kiss. Remembering set the positive tone for the weekend."

When was the first time you remember having romantic feelings for each other?

Favorite Dates

What were your favorite dates before you were married? We had many, and they were usually inexpensive because we were both in college and usually broke. One date stands out in our minds—it was fun but that's not why we remember it. It was summer and Dave was leaving the next day to go to Italy to spend a couple of months with his family (his dad was with NATO in Naples, Italy).

On this memorable date we went hiking in the north Georgia mountains. It was a glorious day, tinged with a bit of sadness at the thought of spending the summer apart. So we decided to make a memory scrapbook. Dave picked a beautiful leaf to go in our scrapbook. It was a day we would definitely remember.

Dave left the next day. Claudia was not only sad, but she also began to itch. Then the rash appeared. Yelp! Boy Scout Dave Arp flunked! He had given Claudia a poison oak leaf! We won't bore you with the details, but to this day Claudia is super sensitive to poison oak, so we remember that date, but not for the romance!

When we talk about our favorite dates, we think of Dave's grandmother. She owned a yellow 1958 Pontiac and generously lent it to her grandson who had no wheels of his own. Claudia lived in the country and the last half mile to her home was a dirt road. Dave remembers washing and spit-shining the yellow Pontiac, only to have it covered with dust by the time he arrived to pick Claudia up for their date. But did we have fun in that car! It took us to all kinds of interesting places, including the mountain/poison oak/picnic date!

What were your favorite dates before you were married?

Keep a list; you may want to do some of these things again as an old married couple! (You could star those dates that you think would be fun to repeat.)

Will I? You Will?! We Do!

Take a few minutes now and talk about your engagement and preparation for your wedding and wedding day. We were both in college (Claudia was in her junior year at the University of Georgia, and Dave was a senior at Georgia Tech) and planned to wait until we graduated from college to tie the knot. Then there was a world crisis—the Cuban Missile Crisis. We were sure the world was going to blow up before we ever had the chance to get married, so we accelerated our plans and decided to get married that Christmas in 1962.

Looking back, we are amazed at how supportive and cooperative our parents were. Dave's parents were in Italy and spent their Christmas vacation traveling (by way of Africa) just to be at our wedding.

Claudia's mom went into overdrive helping with all the wedding plans, and Aunt Annie helped to make the wedding cake. Eight weeks even by today's standards is not very long to plan a church wedding, but we did it! However, after the ceremony, we wondered, what do we do now? How do you build a marriage? We had more commitment than knowledge or know-how, but together, we plodded through those early years. Thirty-one years later, we are amazed at our ignorance—and God's grace!

Talk through and record your best memories of your engagement and wedding.

The Honeymoon

What do you remember from your honeymoon? We only had one weekend for our honeymoon and went to Gatlinburg, Tennessee in the Great Smoky Mountains. This was *before* it was the honeymoon spot of the Southeast. We're embarrassed to tell you how unprepared we were for our honeymoon. We didn't even know about K-Y Jelly!

Our honeymoon was sort of like our first kiss. No real bells and whistles, but it didn't matter. We were together. We were married. We had a lifetime ahead of us to learn how to love each other. We did go buy some K-Y Jelly!

What are your best memories from your honeymoon?

First Christmas

Do you remember your first Christmas together? We remember our first Christmas—well, no, actually we really don't specifically remember it! We were moving from Atlanta, Georgia, to Athens, Georgia, so Claudia could complete her studies at the University of Georgia. Our anniversary comes three days after Christmas, and we actually completed our move on our first anniversary. What stands out in our memory is driving down a main street in Atlanta and realizing our mattress had just fallen off the truck and landed in the middle of Briarcliff Road! We had to stop and carry our mattress back to the truck and try to do a better job of securing it. Yes, we got many strange looks! Our anniversary dinner consisted of driving through the takeout window of a fast-food restaurant!

Our second Christmas was actually the first Christmas together that we really remember. College days were finally behind us, and we had just arrived in Germany at the invitation of Uncle Sam. Actually, Dave had arrived in September. Claudia remained in Athens to complete her last quarter of college.

What a reunion! Claudia's prop flight had mechanical problems and was twenty-four hours late. We arrived in Karlsruhe late on Christmas Eve and got one of the last Christmas trees available. We also got the last of the Christmas tree decorations at the Post Exchange. All Christmas tree lights were long gone, but that didn't matter. Our love for each other and the joy of being together again "lit up our lives." (We still have some of those same Christmas tree decorations!) To this day, one of our favorite songs is "You Light Up My Life."

On Christmas day we dined with new Army friends and sang Christmas carols together as we meandered through our new neighborhood in the snow. Now that's one Christmas we remember!

Now talk about your first Christmas—or the first one you remember (positively)!

First Anniversary

What do you remember about your first anniversary? We've already told you about ours. For some reason—maybe it's the time of the year we got married—anniversaries usually don't work out that well for us. Our second anniversary was no exception.

Dave wanted to impress Claudia, so he drove her in the snow and ice to a famous restaurant in a little German village. The only problem, our anniversary fell on a Monday and that was the *ruhetag* for that restaurant. In English that means it's closed for that day. By the time we got back to Karlsruhe, everything had closed, so we had leftovers.

Now together, remember your first (or first positive) anniversary.

Most Hilarious or Least Romantic Moment

What was your most hilarious or least romantic moment? After more than thirty years, it's hard to isolate just one, but we both remember one of our *romantic getaways* when we found a dead mouse in the Jacuzzi! That did us in for the evening. Another hilarious moment was when we were dating. Dave was telling Claudia good night at her front door and he said, "I'm going to give you a passionate kiss." To which Claudia replied, "Right under my mother's bedroom window?"

What are some of your most hilarious or least romantic moments?

Most Romantic Moment

What was your most romantic moment? Claudia would have to say the time Dave kidnapped her—our boys were his accomplices—and whisked her away to a lovely little hotel in the middle of the Vienna Woods. The surprise element and the fact that Dave took the initiative added to the romance factor!

Dave remembers the first summer we were married. He was at Army ROTC camp and Claudia was back at the University of Georgia for a quick summer quarter. She was living in the Home Management House, part of her requirement for a degree in home economics. As the house did not accommodate married students, Dave, as the responsible adult, had to sign Claudia out for the weekend. But when he tried to sign us in at a local motel, no one believed we were married. He doesn't know if it was being considered "not married" by the motel staff, or the fact that we had been apart for several weeks, or if it was the negligé he surprised Claudia with—whatever it was, he remembers that as one of our *all-time* romantic moments.

Now talk about your own most romantic moments. (You're not limited to just one!)

Places We Have Lived

Revisit in your mind all the different places you have lived. We've already told you about two of the places we have lived. Our third major move was to Tacoma, Washington. We arrived just a few weeks before our first son was born. From there we moved to Atlanta, Knoxville,

Germany, Austria, Knoxville. Dave's motto was, "Marry me and see the world." For a small-town girl like Claudia, life with Dave has been a real trip.

Now retrack your own marriage geography. Many couples tell us they have moved far more than we have. (Actually, we are back in the house we lived in before we lived in Europe. How's that for stability!)

Talk about the different places you have lived.

Happiest Memories

Now share two or three of your happiest times together. One time we especially remember was the week we spent alone in Switzerland when we were developing our Marriage Alive Workshop. Our Swiss friends, Ben and Barbara, were on vacation and lent us their lovely home right on Lake Zurich. We remember eating on their veranda and watching the sun set. We also remember that wonderful feeling of being totally alone and totally relaxed with each other.

Each morning we worked hard on our workshop, and each afternoon we played hard! We won't tell you all the things we did, but we had our own private lab for our session on "Building a Creative Love Life." (On page 37, we're passing on some suggestions for your own creative time for loving each other.)

What are some of the times you've felt the closest?

NOTE: If you have read through these pages before sharing your own memories, turn to pages 41–42 and tear them out. (We realize that may hurt a little bit. It won't be so hard if you are a "creative tearer," but if you prefer, use a pen knife or scissors and do a neat and tidy job.) Mark this page and later we'll meet you back here!

Now that you have had a chance to revisit some of your best memories, it's time to move to the present and affirm your friendship and love for each other.

A TIME FOR FRIENDS AND LOVERS

Now is the time to relax and affirm your commitment to each other. The following activity comes with no pressure, no expectations, no right or wrong answers or actions. It is a time for you to simply relax and enjoy being with your best pal and lover. We want you to love each other in a nondemanding way.

Nondemand loving means just that. This is your time to totally relax with each other. First, you will have the opportunity to come up with your own list of ways to touch and love each other that are low-key, nonthreatening, and lead nowhere. Therapists call this *nondemand touching* and often recommend it to couples who want to improve their sexual relationship. It's a good exercise for a couple who simply wants to enjoy each other without any pressure.

What if one person wants to add something to the list that the other is uncomfortable with? Respect your mate and honor his or her wishes by leaving it off the list and not discussing it. It is not a rejection of you. The guiding principle is that *both* agree that what is listed, *both* would enjoy and feel no pressure to perform. If you are truly trying to please your mate, then concentrate on things you are both enthusiastic about.

Nondemand Loving

From couples who have used this evening exercise on their *Ultimate Marriage Builder* getaway, we pass on some of the things they enjoyed. Use their list as a catalyst to unleash your own creativity.

__ Give a sixty-second hug.

__ Scratch your mate's back.

__ Take a stroll in the moonlight.

__ Go swimming. (If it is totally private you could go skinny-dipping.)

__ Kiss your mate in five different places.

__ Wash your mate's hair.

__ Sing a love song to your mate.

__ Give a back rub.

__ Give a full body massage.

__ Dance together to *your song*.

__ Give a foot rub.

__ Sleep in each other's arms by the fire.

__ Share your favorite dessert and hold hands across the table.

___ Light a fire, turn off the lights, light candles, listen to old records, and just cuddle.

You can check the ones you both would enjoy and add others if you think of them.

Tear out or photocopy the coupons on pages 39–40 and write out the ideas from your list that you like the most. Cut them out in individual strips and put them in a jar, envelope, or bowl. If you brought a small box or container, you can use it now. Remember to leave out any you are uncomfortable with.

Time to Rekindle the Spark

Now's the time to use your crystal glasses or china cups for a romantic snack. Light some of the candles you brought along, put on your favorite CD or cassette tape—you may even want to play *your song*. Relax and enjoy the feeling of your mate's loving but nondemanding touch.

We'll leave you alone now, with your container of fun. The eager beaver can draw first and the other can give the hug, kiss, or whatever.

Remember this is nonpressure loving! You may be so exhausted that you simply fall asleep together. That's okay; we've got a great day planned for you tomorrow, and we want you to be rested. Good night from the Arps!

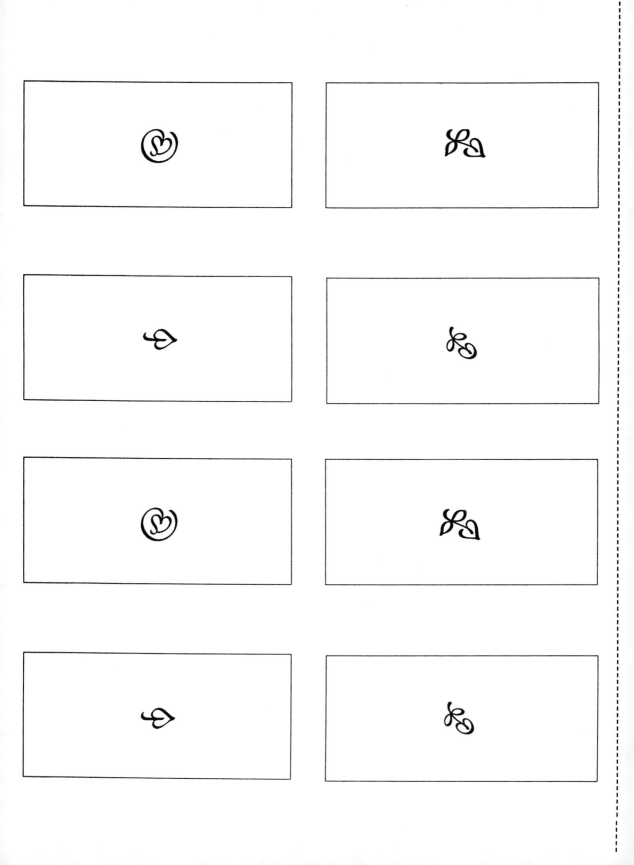

Rekindling the Spark

First Memories: _____
_____
_____

First Date: _____
_____
_____

First Kiss: _____
_____
_____

Favorite Dates: _____
_____
_____

Will I? You Will?! We Do!: _____
_____
_____

The Honeymoon: _____
_____
_____

First Christmas: _____
_____
_____

First Anniversary: _____

_____

_____

Most Hilarious or Least Romantic Moment: _____

_____

_____

Most Romantic Moment: _____

_____

_____

Places You Have Lived: _____

_____

_____

Happiest Memories: _____

_____

_____

Now that you have had a chance to revisit some of your best memories, it's time to move to the present and affirm your friendship with and love for each other, so return to page 36 for a time for friends and lovers.

_____

Vive La Différence

Good morning! We hope you enjoyed your first *Ultimate Marriage Builder* adventure. We hope you revived good memories and maybe even made some new ones!

You may want to get another cup of coffee or tea, make yourselves comfortable, and get ready to look at how you can enrich your relationship through understanding and benefiting from the ways you are different from each other.

OUR STORY

"Opposites attract," goes the old adage. Is this true in your experience? What differences still amaze you in your marriage? We are very different from each other, and sometimes those differences not only attract us to each other, but also create tension in our relationship. For the first few years of our marriage we tried changing each other, and it just didn't work.

When we think back to our premarriage days, it was the ways we were different that initially attracted us to each other. Claudia still remembers being attracted to this laid-back, easygoing guy who had all the time in the world to listen to her. Dave liked Claudia's high energy level, endless ideas, and constant chatter. It was a great match. Right? Well, yes and no. Yes, before marriage, when both romance and hormones abounded! Every day was exciting. Dave's calmness and attentiveness complemented Claudia's three-ring circus of activity. Our rose-tinted glasses helped us appreciate our differences, and we naturally seemed to concentrate on the positive.

Then came the wedding and the honeymoon, closely followed by the real life struggles of a young couple on a limited budget trying to balance work and complete college at the same time. Romance was still present, but now reality entered. Claudia redefined Dave's laid-backness as lack of motivation. No matter how many firecrackers she set under Dave, he was still slow and steady. Dave couldn't understand why Claudia was so introspective and analytical, and soon tired of this bundle of activity he had married. Oh, for one quiet evening!

Fast forward eight years. Add a quiver of little boys and all the responsibilities of parenting. Life just got more complicated and our differences more pronounced. About this time we made a job change that required us to take a battery of psychological tests. We still remember the day we filled out those tests. Dave nonchalantly checked off his answers while watching a football game on television. Claudia was intense, cross-checking her answers for consistency.

The next week we were interviewed by Dr. Howard Blandau, a psychologist. He sat at his desk, looking at our test results. "Dave, here are your strong points." As he listed them, Dave began to feel better and better. He went on, "Here are the areas in which you are weak." That wasn't nearly as enjoyable for Dave to hear, but the psychologist was right on target!

Then he went through the same procedure with Claudia, listing her strengths and weaknesses. Looking at both of us he said, "Dave and Claudia, here are the areas you agree on, and here are the areas in which you tend to have problems." He could have been a fly on our walls the past year. He didn't miss anything. Our respect for those tests went up about three hundred percent. Then he gave us one of the most beneficial challenges of our lives: "You've probably noticed, Dave, that your weak areas are Claudia's strengths, and Claudia, your weak areas are Dave's strengths. If you will allow each other to operate in your areas of strength and not be threatened by the other, you have the potential for being a terrific team."

We would like to tell you we applied his advice instantly—but we can't! It's hard to admit openly that your weakness is your mate's strength and vice versa. It took time and practice, and at times we still struggle, but we continue to take Dr. Blandau's challenge seriously. It's helped us to be a stronger team, and it can help you too!

Soon it will be your turn to pick your own strengths. Do you already see areas where your differences give balance to your marriage team? Is there an area where you are so similar that you need to compensate? For instance, if you're both the serious type, how can you add a little humor and fun to your marriage?

Our goal is to benefit from each other's strengths and appreciate each other's differences. Take it from us, this is one goal worth working toward. How do we know? Years later we retook the same tests and sat down with the same psychologist. The results? We had actually learned from each other. Our weak areas were not as weak. We were a stronger team. Plus, we definitely were having more fun. Now we challenge you to prove it for yourself. Work for unity in your diversity, and you too can appreciate "vive la différence!"

APPRECIATE YOUR DIFFERENCES

You are getting ready to embark on an experience that can greatly enhance your marriage. You will have the opportunity to understand each other more clearly and appreciate the strengths each of you bring to your marriage partnership. However, you should proceed with care. Looking at each other's strengths and weaknesses can be an open door to hurt feelings. If your mate happens to miss mentioning some of your positive qualities, assume he or she is just picking those that are in focus right then. We know you are going to be amazed when you see at the end of this exercise what a strong marriage team you have!

Here's what one wife had to say about it: "It was great to realize that couples who are as different as we are can have a joyful, fun, and productive marriage. This exercise is great. It's always hard to get my wonderful, laid-back husband motivated to do something that looks like work, but once he got into it, he was very motivated."

Now It's Your Turn

For your convenience, we are including two copies of this exercise. Tear or cut out the next 16 pages. Later you can add them to your notebook or folder. You won't have to worry about someone else's thumbing through your book and reading the *personal* entries you have made. Now, just follow the instructions and cautions within the exercise.

Picture Your Marriage Partnership

Her Copy

In this exercise we want to help you better understand each other and your marriage partnership. This will help you appreciate your strengths as a marital team and work together on areas in which you may be weak.

Part I: Picking Your Traits

The following is a list of descriptive words. Individually, go through the list and initial the words that tend to describe you. Then initial the words that tend to describe your mate. (Some words may describe both of you. If so, put both initials.)

—— Spontaneous	—— Optimistic	—— Friendly
—— Enthusiastic	—— Talkative	—— Responsive
—— Charismatic	—— Fun	—— Strong-Willed
—— Adventurous	—— Confident	—— Decisive
—— Quick Thinking	—— Competitive	—— Tenacious
—— Productive	—— Creative	—— Deep Thinker
—— Introspective	—— Idealistic	—— Perfectionist
—— Detail-Oriented	—— Sensitive	—— Self-Disciplined
—— Stabilizing	—— Dry Humor	—— Practical
—— Good-Natured	—— Diplomatic	—— Peaceful
—— Consistent	—— Easygoing	

A WORD OF CAUTION FROM THE ARPS: As you compare your perceptions with each other, remember why you are doing this exercise: to help you better understand each other and the combined strengths you bring to your marriage partnership.

Determine to remain positive. Refrain from assigning labels or from giving negative feedback. Focus on strengths. Just because you may not see yourself the same way your mate sees you doesn't have to be negative.

For example, one husband and wife who did this exercise both checked themselves as being deep thinkers and introspective but failed to check that the other was too! Their only crime was being so caught up in their own introspection that they overlooked those traits in their mate. (Both were obviously correct in their assessments of themselves!)

Another caution: Choose your words carefully. Frame them as positively as you can. When April told Elliot, "Honey, you're just there," she meant it as a compliment—that he was dependable, steady, and there for her! It took a little convincing for Elliot to see it that way.

Should you slip and become angry, stop this exercise and go to the Mini Marriage Builder, "Learning to Process Anger," on page 147. This is *preventive* advice, and a word to the wise beforehand is sufficient.

Compare your descriptions on page 47 with each other and discuss the following questions:

1. In what ways are you very much alike (those words initialed for both of you)?

_____

_____

2. Now go back and circle the four words that best describe yourself.

3. Do you see ways you balance each other?

_____

_____

_____

_____

_____

 NOTE: If this exercise has been fun to this point, keep going. If you are struggling with this one, we suggest you save the last part for another time. This is a nondemand exercise. Either of you has the right to say, "Let's do something else!"

Part II: Comparing Your Strengths

Many different grids and personality charts are popular today. Like the psychological test we took years ago, they can be helpful in learning about ourselves. In a marriage, partners tend to play particular roles based on the strengths of their personalities and/or others' expectations of them. The next part of this exercise will help you evaluate your roles based on the strengths of your personality.

Compare your list from Part I with the following survey. In each category initial the words you initialed in Part I. Then add up the number of initialed words for each of you in each category.

Category A: The Popular Sanguine, emotional, socializer, expressive, influencer are all popular names given to people with the following traits:

	Total No. for Him	Total No. for Her
____ Spontaneous		
____ Optimistic		
____ Friendly	_____	_____
____ Enthusiastic		
____ Talkative		
____ Responsive		
____ Charismatic		
____ Fun		

Category B: The Powerful Choleric, director, driver, dominant are all popular names given to people with these traits:

	Total No. for Him	Total No. for Her
____ Strong-Willed		
____ Adventurous		
____ Confident	_____	_____
____ Decisive		
____ Quick Thinking		
____ Competitive		
____ Tenacious		
____ Productive		

Category C: The Perfect Melancholy, thinker, analytical, cautious are all popular names given to people with these traits:

	Total No. for Him	Total No. for Her
___ Creative		
___ Deep Thinker	_____	_____
___ Introspective		
___ Idealistic		
___ Perfectionist		
___ Detail-Oriented		
___ Sensitive		
___ Self-Disciplined		

Category D: The Peaceful Phlegmatic, amiable, relater, steady are all popular names given to people with these traits:

	Total No. for Him	Total No. for Her
___ Stabilizing		
___ Dry Humor	_____	_____
___ Practical		
___ Good-Natured		
___ Diplomatic		
___ Peaceful		
___ Consistent		
___ Easygoing		

Now discuss together:

1. In which of the four categories are we most alike? How can we make this work for us?

We are most alike in category A. Dave had a six and Claudia a five. As we talked about it, we realized this is why we work together so well in settings like media interviews, speaking engagements, and work-shops. One of us doesn't outshine the other, and we are a true partner-ship. We are both spontaneous, friendly, and talkative—all important qualities in relating to others.

Now look at the category(s) in which you are most alike and talk about how you can make this work for you:

_____

_____

_____

2. In which of the four categories are we most different?

We are the most different in category B and category D. Claudia has category B covered with seven to Dave's one, while Dave leads in category D with eight to Claudia's two. Claudia is the driver, while Dave is the pacer and keeps us on an even course.

Now look at how you are most different. Discuss the following questions: How can we approach our differences in a constructive and realistic way? How can we be more productive in these areas? How can we pull together?

_____

_____

_____

_____

3. Choose one couple strength to celebrate.

As they did this exercise on their weekend, Lois and Kevin realized that they both bring humor to their family, and with two teenagers this is a real asset. They decided to celebrate their ability to laugh and submit a video to *The Home Video Bloopers* contest.

What strength do you choose to celebrate?

_____

_____

_____

4. Choose one couple weakness to constructively work on.

Realizing areas of weakness is the first step in learning to compensate for them.

Bob and Frances realized on their getaway that they both like neatness, but are weak in carry-through. Bob told us, "I realize I can't criticize Frances for leaving her towel on the bathroom floor when it is lying next to my towel. We decided we would work on this one together. I have a tendency to project my problem or weakness onto Frances—especially when it is a weakness she shares. So until we can afford a maid, we are going to keep working on this one!"

Now pick one area of mutual weakness that you both want to work on. Talk about what you can realistically do that would be productive and constructive.

_____

_____

_____

_____

Picture Your Marriage Partnership

His Copy

In this exercise we want to help you better understand each other and your marriage partnership. This will help you appreciate your strengths as a marital team and work together on areas in which you may be weak.

Part I: Picking Your Traits

The following is a list of descriptive words. Individually, go through the list and initial the words that tend to describe you. Then initial the words that tend to describe your mate. (Some words may describe both of you. If so, put both initials.)

___ Spontaneous	___ Optimistic	___ Friendly
___ Enthusiastic	___ Talkative	___ Responsive
___ Charismatic	___ Fun	___ Strong-Willed
___ Adventurous	___ Confident	___ Decisive
___ Quick Thinking	___ Competitive	___ Tenacious
___ Productive	___ Creative	___ Deep Thinker
___ Introspective	___ Idealistic	___ Perfectionist
___ Detail-Oriented	___ Sensitive	___ Self-Disciplined
___ Stabilizing	___ Dry Humor	___ Practical
___ Good-Natured	___ Diplomatic	___ Peaceful
___ Consistent	___ Easygoing	

A WORD OF CAUTION FROM THE ARPS: As you compare your perceptions with each other, remember why you are doing this exercise: to help you better understand each other and the combined strengths you bring to your marriage partnership.

Determine to remain positive. Refrain from assigning labels or from giving negative feedback. Focus on strengths. Just because you may not see yourself the same way your mate sees you doesn't have to be negative.

For example, one husband and wife who did this exercise both checked themselves as being deep thinkers and introspective but failed to check that the other was too! Their only crime was being so caught up in their introspection that they overlooked those traits in their mate. (Both were obviously correct in their assessments of themselves!)

Another caution: Choose your words carefully. Frame them as positively as you can. When April told Elliot, "Honey, you're just there," she meant it as a compliment—that he was dependable, steady, and there for her! It took a little convincing for Elliot to see it that way.

Should you slip and become angry, stop this exercise and go to the Mini Marriage Builder, "Learning to Process Anger," on page 147. This is *preventive* advice, and a word to the wise beforehand is sufficient.

Compare your descriptions on page 55 with each other and discuss the following questions:

1. In what ways are you very much alike (those words initialed for both of you)?

_____
_____

2. Now go back and circle the four words that best describe yourself.

3. Do you see ways you balance each other?

_____
_____
_____
_____
_____

NOTE: If this exercise has been fun to this point, keep going. If you are struggling with this one, we suggest you save the last part for another time. This is a nondemand exercise. Either of you has the right to say, "Let's do something else!"

Part II: Comparing Your Strengths

Many different grids and personality charts are popular today. Like the psychological test we took years ago, they can be helpful in learning about ourselves. In a marriage, partners tend to play particular roles based on the strengths of their personalities and/or others' expectations of them. The next part of this exercise will help you evaluate your roles based on the strengths of your personality.

The Getaway

Compare your list from Part I with the following survey. In each category initial the words you initialed in Part I. Then add up the number of initialed words for each of you in each category.

Category A: The Popular Sanguine, emotional, socializer, expressive, influencer are all popular names given to people with the following traits:

___ Spontaneous	
___ Optimistic	
___ Friendly	
___ Enthusiastic	
___ Talkative	
___ Responsive	
___ Charismatic	
___ Fun	

Total No. for Him   Total No. for Her

_____   _____

Category B: The Powerful Choleric, director, driver, dominant are all popular names given to people with these traits:

Total No. for Him   Total No. for Her

_____   _____

___ Strong-Willed
___ Adventurous
___ Confident
___ Decisive
___ Quick Thinking
___ Competitive
___ Tenacious
___ Productive

Category C: The Perfect Melancholy, thinker, analytical, cautious are all popular names given to people with these traits:

___ Creative   Total No. for Him   Total No. for Her
___ Deep Thinker
___ Introspective   _____   _____
___ Idealistic
___ Perfectionist
___ Detail-Oriented
___ Sensitive
___ Self-Disciplined

Category D: The Peaceful Phlegmatic, amiable, relater, steady are all popular names given to people with these traits:

___ Stabilizing   Total No. for Him   Total No. for Her
___ Dry Humor
___ Practical   _____   _____
___ Good-Natured
___ Diplomatic
___ Peaceful
___ Consistent
___ Easygoing

Now discuss together:

1. In which of the four categories are we most alike? How can we make this work for us?

    We are most alike in category A. Dave had a six and Claudia a five.

As we talked about it, we realized this is why we work together so well in settings like media interviews, speaking engagements, and workshops. One of us doesn't outshine the other, and we are a true partnership. We are both spontaneous, friendly, and talkative—all important qualities in relating to others.

Now look at the category(s) in which you are most alike and talk about how you can make this work for you:

_____

_____

_____

2. In which of the four categories are we most different?

We are the most different in category B and category D. Claudia has category B covered with seven to Dave's one, while Dave leads in category D with eight to Claudia's two. Claudia is the driver, while Dave is the pacer and keeps us on an even course.

Now look at how you are most different. Discuss the following questions: How can we approach our differences in a constructive and realistic way? How can we be more productive in these areas? How can we pull together?

_____

_____

_____

_____

_____

3. Choose one couple strength to celebrate.

As they did this exercise on their weekend, Lois and Kevin realized that they both bring humor to their family, and with two teenagers this is a real asset. They decided to celebrate their ability to laugh and submit a video to *The Home Video Bloopers* contest.

What strength do you choose to celebrate?

_____

_____

_____

4. Choose one couple weakness to constructively work on.

Realizing areas of weakness is the first step in learning to compensate for them.

Bob and Frances realized on their getaway that they both like neatness, but are weak in carry-through. Bob told us, "I realize I can't criticize Frances for leaving her towel on the bathroom floor when it is lying next to my towel. We decided we would work on this one together. I have a tendency to project my problem or weakness onto Frances—especially when it is a weakness she shares. So until we can afford a maid, we are going to keep working on this one!"

Now pick one area of mutual weakness that you both want to work on. Talk about what you can realistically do that would be productive and constructive.

_____

_____

_____

61

OPTIONAL MINI MARRIAGE BUILDER SUGGESTIONS
For more opportunities to talk about "Vive la Différence" see:
"Defining Your Masculinity and Femininity," *page 112*
"The Discovery Exercise," *page 113*
"Great Expectations," *page 119*

Celebrate Your Marriage Partnership

We hope you have enjoyed looking at your marriage partnership and that you have made progress accepting and understanding both your strengths and weaknesses. We encourage you to continue to look for ways to celebrate your marriage.

This afternoon, you will get to celebrate with a fun exercise, "Fresh Air—Talking Together." You're on your own until then!

Chapter Five

SATURDAY AFTERNOON

Fun and Fresh Air

"That Saturday afternoon we spent hours just talking. We relaxed, ate ice cream, bought T-shirts, and walked barefooted along Lake Superior. We splashed with our feet in the cold water and decided we would take up sailing one day! When Sunday came, we didn't want to go home!"

Best friends, married four years, expecting first child

Sound like fun? This couple's conversation started with the exercise you are going to do in just a few minutes. It's more than fun—it's vital to a marriage's health. A recent study of 351 couples (married fifteen or more years) was conducted to determine how marriages survive and thrive in this turbulent world.[2] Those with enduring, happy marriages agree on why they get along so well. When asked, "What keeps a marriage going?" the top reason given (the same for both husbands and wives) was, "My spouse is my best friend." The next six reasons (also the same for both mates) were:

- I like my spouse as a person.
- Marriage is a long-term commitment.
- Marriage is sacred.

• We agree on aims and goals.

• My spouse has grown more interesting.

• I want our relationship to succeed.

What keeps your marriage going? For us, we'd have to say the time we spend talking and doing things together. Our refreshing times usually begin with conversation, so we've put together a communication questionnaire to facilitate yours. But first, we have some tips for you.

COMMUNICATION TIPS
• Avoid "You" statements and "Why" questions. They tend to be attacking.
• Practice starting your sentences with "I." "I" statements are much safer.
• Avoid using absolute statements like "You never. . . . You always. . . ."
• No garbage dumping or bringing up past hurts or past indiscretions. These need to be dealt with, but on a weekend that is designed to be a positive growing experience, couples can get sidetracked by these and find it hard to regain a positive perspective. Make a list of major things that need to be dealt with and later seek help from a counselor, pastor, or caring professional.

NOTE: If you are unsure how to dialogue on a feelings level, then before you begin this exercise, turn to the Mini Marriage Builder, Four Styles of Communication, page 137, and work through it. Then you will be ready for "Fun and Fresh Air."

FRESH AIR

To get the most out of this exercise take a few minutes and individually write down your answers to each question. Be honest, yet never unkind. Let us encourage you to be specific and positive.

After you have filled out the questionnaire, share your answers with each other question-by-question. You may want to alternate who goes first each time.

If you are walkers like us, you may want to go for a walk as you share your answers. If one of you doesn't like to write, simply talk through the questions together. The purpose of this time is to help you communicate on a more intimate level.

Now turn to the next page, tear out the pages with the questions, and begin.

Fresh Air—Talking Together

Her Copy

Couples rarely have difficulty expressing their feelings when they are angry or upset, but often find it difficult to share their more tender feelings. This questionnaire helps you do just that.

1. List three things your mate does that please you. Be specific. Include little things or big things. (Dave is really pleased when Claudia goes through the horizontal files on her desk, and Claudia really likes it when Dave surprises her with their favorite Chinese take-out food.)

_____

_____

_____

2. List three things you would like your mate to do more often. Be positive and specific. (Claudia would like for Dave to be the one to say more often, "Let's go for a walk." Dave likes surprises, such as a kidnap date to the dollar cinema.)

_____

_____

_____

3. List three things you think your mate would like you to do more

often. (We both would love for the other to volunteer to clean the
kitchen and take out the garbage! We also like back rubs.)

_____

_____

_____

4. In what ways would you like your mate to let you know you are
appreciated? (Hugs and kisses work for us!)

_____

_____

_____

5. When you are in need of support, what do you like your mate to do?
(Claudia says, "Listen! Listen! Listen!" Dave at times wants a little
space and for Claudia just to be there and not say anything.)

_____

_____

_____

6. What are some of the milestones of your marriage? A milestone
would be a special event that significantly affected the direction of your
lives together. Explain why it was a milestone. Perhaps this weekend
will be one of your marriage milestones!

_____

_____

_____

Fresh Air—Talking Together

His Copy

Couples rarely have difficulty expressing their feelings when they are angry or upset, but often find it difficult to share their more tender feelings. This questionnaire helps you do just that.

1. List three things your mate does that please you. Be specific. Include little things or big things. (Dave is really pleased when Claudia goes through the horizontal files on her desk, and Claudia really likes it when Dave surprises her with their favorite Chinese takeout food.)

_____

_____

_____

2. List three things you would like your mate to do more often. Be positive and specific. (Claudia would like for Dave to be the one to say more often, "Let's go for a walk." Dave likes surprises, such as a kidnap date to the dollar cinema.)

_____

_____

_____

3. List three things you think your mate would like you to do more

often. (We both would love for the other to volunteer to clean the kitchen and take out the garbage! We also like back rubs.)

_____

_____

_____

4. In what ways would you like your mate to let you know you are appreciated? (Hugs and kisses work for us!)

_____

_____

_____

5. When you are in need of support, what do you like your mate to do? (Claudia says, "Listen! Listen! Listen!" Dave at times wants a little space and for Claudia just to be there and not say anything.)

_____

_____

_____

6. What are some of the milestones of your marriage? A milestone would be a special event that significantly affected the direction of your lives together. Explain why it was a milestone. Perhaps this weekend will be one of your marriage milestones!

_____

_____

_____

OPTIONAL MENU MARRIAGE BUILDER SUGGESTIONS:
For More Talking see:
"How Do I Feel When," *page 139*
"Daily Sharing Times," *page 132*
"Becoming Close Companions," *page 142*

TIME FOR FUN

Once you finish your exercise, we suggest you spend the rest of the afternoon doing whatever you want to do. For Dave, that would include napping. Claudia may get Dave on the tennis court for a couple of sets. If not, she'll probably curl up with the book she brought along.

This is your time to do whatever you want. You don't have to spend every minute with each other. You may want to have some time alone with God to read the scriptures, pray, write in a journal, or whatever.

If you were too tired last night to fully take advantage of your time for friends and lovers, you could start wherever you left off. Then you will be all primed for tonight's time for "Romancing Your Mate!"

Chapter Six

SATURDAY EVENING

Romancing Your Mate

What conjures up romance in your mind? Kathy's husband, Gary, is the ultimate "romantic," but even his best-laid plans sometimes go awry. They had just finished a lovely dinner by candlelight at their favorite restaurant. It was one of those evenings where you just take things slow and aren't in a hurry to get home, so Gary took the long way home, driving by the beach. "What could be more romantic for a middle-aged married couple," Gary thought, "than to stop and park on the beach with your wife on a moonlit night?"

Kathy, adventurous herself, was enjoying this scenario, when they noticed blue lights flashing behind them. "Just what do you think you are doing?" asked the police officer.

"I'm kissing my wife," replied Gary.

To which the officer replied, "If this is your wife, then you have your own bedroom, and I suggest you take her there!" The officer just didn't understand.

Bedrooms are wonderful places, but romance thrives on doing the unexpected, and for Gary and Kathy on that evening, the beach was part of the romantic interlude! We do understand the police officer's concern; parking isn't the safest thing to do, but that doesn't need to stop you from being creative and doing something unexpected!

DO THE UNEXPECTED

One key to keeping romance alive is maintaining a spirit of surprise and inventiveness. Lucy and Frank (not their real names) were on an austere budget while trying to get out of debt. Their love life had been a little austere too, but Lucy decided to do something about it. Their good friends were away on vacation and left the keys to their house with Lucy. Lucy made her plans. Her younger sister agreed to stay with their children for an evening. She called Frank and said she would pick him up after work. She then rented an old black and white romantic movie and packed a picnic dinner complete with candles and a checkered tablecloth.

Frank was waiting on the corner for Lucy, not sure what she had up her sleeve. "Honey," Lucy said as Frank got in the car, "I just want to tell you, I don't have on any underwear and we're not going home."

Outrageous? Wacky? Perhaps, but definitely romantic!

NOTE: If you find it uncomfortable to talk about your sexual relationship, before you continue in this evening of "Romancing Your Mate," take a short detour and turn to page 169 and talk through the Mini Marriage Builder, "Learning to Talk about the 'S' Word." Then continue with this chapter.

BUST OUT OF THE RUT

Stop and think about why Frank and Lucy's adventure was so romantic. One, they jolted their established patterns. Two, there was the element of surprise. Three, Lucy did something completely out of character (not wearing any underwear!).

Now, stop and think about what you can do to jolt your own established patterns. What could you do that is a little out of character? If you need some help in fanning the flames of your love life, we suggest Dr. Clifford and Joyce Penners' lighthearted, fun, and sometimes wacky book, *52 Ways to Have Fun, Fantastic Sex* (Thomas Nelson, 1994).

If you are having major sexual problems, their book or this one won't fix them, but if your sex life is just in a rut, this may be just what you need. "Wackiness," the Penners write, "often helps loosen up and lighten the deadly serious business of sex."[3]

However, just as no chef expects everyone to like every item on the menu, you probably won't find every idea for putting a glow in your love life appealing. If any of the suggestions in *52 Ways to Have Fun, Fantastic Sex*, or in this chapter (or from any other source) will cause distance, turmoil, and tension, please skip it. It's great to stretch and grow, but never when it's against your own will and choice.

We've talked a lot about nondemand loving. Demands take all the fun out of sex. So if any experience feels like a demand, communicate that to your spouse. Try those suggestions that you both respond to positively. Experiment with others that are on the edge of your limits. Make adaptations. Stretch yourself to be sillier than is common for the two of you. You will be on your way to having fun, fantastic sex!

GIFTS FROM THE HEART

Remember our suggestion to bring gifts for each other? Now is a great time to share them. One wife on their getaway presented her husband with boxer shorts with hand-painted hearts all over them. Later he said real love was wearing those boxer shorts to work, because they were the only pair he had that was clean!

To our Marriage Encounter friends, why not christen new matching T-shirts. Think of the memories! We love pulling out our matching terry cloth robes that we reserve for our times away. Whatever adds to your pleasure is what you should do!

BUBBLE BATH FOR TWO

Bubble baths for two usually get a big billing in books and magazine articles for married lovers. Even though we both prefer showers, a bubble bath for two can be fun. If you light the scented candles you brought along, you can bathe by candlelight. Another nice touch would be soft music in the background, and you may even want to have close by a tray of refreshments. Whenever we attend the Parade of New Homes, usually in the master bathroom there are a couple of crystal, long-stem glasses all ready to be filled. So fix your own treats. Use your imagination!

SHOWERS OF LOVE

Once when we were speaking at a "Sweetheart's Banquet" in a church, an elderly couple came up to us after our talk. "When we were first married," they told us, "someone suggested we shower together. We tried it, and it was so much fun, we've been showering together every morning since!"

Romance isn't reserved just for the young. But to keep romance alive over the long haul of a marriage requires intentional planning. We hope this evening will be a romantic interlude for you, but we also hope it will be a catalyst to future romance.

One couple who attended a Marriage Encounter Weekend after twenty-three years of marriage told us, "We experienced romance again! It is a marvelous freeing experience like reaching the summit of a mountain!"

Our friends, Dave and Jeanie Stanley, past Executive Couple for United Marriage Encounter, and married over forty-five years, give this advice, "Romance doesn't have to die out. It can grow and blossom through all your married years, if you continue to show your love in physical ways, plus loving words and deeds. God designed man and woman to enjoy each other's body in marriage, and we find that enjoyment still growing after forty-five years of marriage."[4]

SEX BY GOD'S DESIGN

God is the one who created us male and female. God is the one who originated sex, and aren't we glad He did!

NOTE: If you're just not sure how you feel about this, we suggest that you pause and read two of the Mini Marriage Builders. Start with "The Bible on Sex," page 171. Then turn to "God in the Bedroom," page 180 for advice from the Penners. After completing these two Mini Marriage Builders, you may continue with "Time for Remembering."

TIME FOR REMEMBERING

We love what the Spanish poet Antonio Machado said:

> I thought the fire was out in my fireplace.
> I stirred the ashes,
> And I burned my hands.

We hope the next exercise will stir up your ashes as you remember together. Talk about what you have done to romance each other. What have you done that was totally unexpected?

_____

_____

_____

What romantic memories do you have from your courtship? Think back to how you used to flirt with each other. If you bring back some of the things you used to do years ago, you may discover all those sparks are still there.

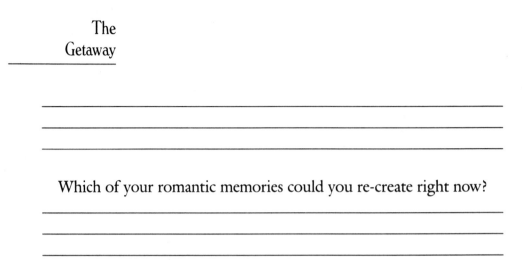

The
Getaway

_____

_____

_____

Which of your romantic memories could you re-create right now?

_____

_____

_____

TIME FOR ROMANCE

Enough from the Arps for one day. This is your evening. If you are in the mood to talk or are looking for other creative suggestions, choose from the Mini Marriage Builders (in the Dessert section), pages 165–183. We recommend the following:

- "Five Tips for Rekindling Your Love," page 182
- "From Good Sex to Great Sex," page 177
- "Granting Three Wishes," page 168

Again we encourage you to choose what interests you and what feels comfortable for you. This is your evening to enjoy. Keep the same attitude of *no pressure* from last evening and enjoy romancing your mate!

We close with a comment from one couple who were just too tired! "We were both so tired from our long week and day that we were pretty tame in our 'Three Wishes.' Actually, we didn't even think of three until Sunday morning. My husband wanted to know if they had a time limit on when they had to be taken." We told them, "That's totally up to you!"

Chapter Seven

SUNDAY

Room to Grow

> Grow old along with me!
> The best is yet to be.

Do Robert Browning's words ring true in your marriage? If your answer is no, don't be discouraged. Wherever you are in your marriage, it can be better tomorrow. Marriage is never static. It's always changing. Perhaps your marriage is changing this weekend. The fact that you are at this point in your own personal encounter tells us you are serious about your relationship and want to, as friends in A.C.M.E. (the Association for Couples in Marriage Enrichment) say, "Make marriages better, beginning with your own!"

THE THREE SIDES OF LOVE

What keeps love growing over the years? Robert S. Trotter, a professor at Yale University, has an interesting theory of love and how we express it.[5] He sees love as a triangle, not the kind of love triangle that involves three people but a triangle whose three sides are intimacy, passion, and commitment. Let's take a closer look.

Intimacy—Intimacy is the emotional aspect of the love triangle. It includes the closeness and sharing in marriage: intimate conversations, sharing our deepest feelings with each other, giving our unconditional support to each other. Intimacy develops slowly over the years, without fanfare; you each become the other's trusted best friend and confidant.

Passion—Passion is the motivational side of love. It's the intense desire to be united physically with the person you love. Unlike intimacy, passion develops quickly. As depicted in the Hollywood soaps, passion is a rapidly growing, hot, heavy experience. You don't even have to know the other person to feel passionate. In a real-life marriage, passion may (and probably will) level off. That doesn't mean it's not there, but you may need to cultivate it.

Commitment—Commitment is the cognitive side of love. It started at nothing when you first met but grew as you got to know each other. Sternberg says commitment is a short-term decision to love another person and a long-term decision to maintain that love. Commitment is one element of love that is desperately missing in many marriages today. Almost half of today's marriages end in divorce.

Balancing Your Triangle

Stop for a moment and look at your own relationship. Do you see the three sides of love functioning in your marriage? Are your sides balanced? How big is your triangle? What would be your ideal triangle? How can you find a comfortable balance?

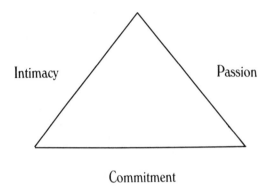

Change for the Better

Remember, we said the marriage relationship is always changing. What really mattered to us in the short run—physical attractiveness, chemistry, romance—may not be what matters most in the long run. Things you thought were kind of cute, over the long haul may begin to grate on you. We continually need to be willing to change and adapt to each other, to forgive each other, and to let our love grow into a mature, lasting love relationship.

Sternberg discovered that among the things that actually increase in importance over the years is simply having a willingness to change in response to each other and to tolerate each other's quirks. In our marriage history of over thirty years, we have learned we can't change each other; we can only change ourselves. But an interesting thing happens: when one of us changes, the other tends to change too.

Research reveals that another thing that becomes increasingly important over the years is the sharing of values, especially religious values.

The things that tend to diminish over the years (this is not very encouraging) are the ability to communicate, physical attractiveness, having good times together, sharing interests, the ability to listen, respect for each other, and romantic love. But this doesn't have to happen to your relationship—especially if you talk to each other.

Do you need to work on one side to bring your relationship more into balance? Discuss your answers to these three questions:

1. Do we need to increase the intimacy in our relationship?

Increasing intimacy might include being willing to express your true feelings to each other, to offer more emotional support, to share your time and selves with each other.

Place your relationship on this scale. Do you agree with each other on where you are on the scale?

Intimacy

Low _____ High

     0   1   2   3   4   5   6   7   8   9   10

2. Do we need more passion in our love life?

More passion might include more getaways like this one, more hugs, more kisses, more tender touches, scheduling more time to love each other. Many people have said to us, "That doesn't sound passionate or romantic to me!" We understand what they are saying, but passion like faith often comes when we step out and take the risk. If you don't plan, passion probably won't happen on its own.

Now, place your relationship on this scale and talk about where you are with your mate.

Passion

Low _____ High

    0   1   2   3   4   5   6   7   8   9   10

3. How can we express a deeper commitment to each other?

Expressing your commitment might include staying in the relationship through the hard times, being faithful to your mate, and being committed to maintaining your love relationship.

Again, place your relationship on this scale and discuss together.

Commitment

Low _____ High

    0   1   2   3   4   5   6   7   8   9   10

Three Biblical Principles

While this triangle illustration comes from research at Yale University, there is a biblical basis for it. A key passage on the foundation of marriage is found in Genesis 2:24: "For this cause a man shall leave his father and his mother, and shall cleave to his wife; and they shall become one flesh" (NASB).

This verse gives three principles basic to a growing, loving marriage relationship: leaving, cleaving, and becoming one flesh. Let's compare these biblical principles with the three sides of love.

Leaving Involves Commitment

Genesis 2:24 describes leaving in the context of leaving your family of origin and forming a new family. It is a picture of a commitment for life. It's also focusing on each other and making other people and things less important.

Cleaving Involves Intimacy

Cleaving to each other gives the picture of commitment that goes beyond just sticking together. It means growing in intimacy—being that one person the other can always count on, being best friends, sharing life on the deepest, most intimate level.

Becoming One Involves Passion

God originated passion and designed it to be played out between husband and wife for all the days of your lives together. He created us male and female and put the potential for passion deep within us. He designed us to experience sexually a unique oneness. It is with God's blessing we can pursue becoming passionate lovers.

EVALUATING YOUR MARRIAGE

Think about your marriage today. Are your three sides out of balance? Do you want to grow in your relationship with each other? You can start by acknowledging where you are right now in your relationship.

For the following exercise, individually write on a separate piece of paper your own observations and then discuss them with each other. When you finish the exercise, put them in your notebook or folder.

From time to time review them and appreciate the progress you are making and the ways you are changing.

FINISHING THE RACE

For a marriage to go the distance, not only do we need to appreciate the past and acknowledge the present, but also we need to plan for the future. Couples who are committed to finishing the race together have a much better chance of realizing their dreams.

For us, faith in God has much to do with our commitment to permanence in our marriage. In 2 Timothy 4:7 Paul speaks of finishing the race: "I have fought the good fight, I have finished the race, I have kept the faith."

If you relate this verse to your marriage, what do you want your marriage to look like at the finish line? Do you know an older couple who have that kind of relationship? We do.

For years our friends and mentors, David and Vera Mace, modeled for us an enriched Christian marriage. We saw in their relationship the

Evaluating Our Marriage

1. Three things that are good about our marriage relationship (for example, a great sense of humor, open communication, and common spiritual values):

_____

_____

_____

_____

_____

_____

2. Three things about our relationship that are good but could be better (for example, handling of finances, spending time together, and sticking to goals):

_____

_____

_____

_____

_____

_____

3. Three things I could do to make our marriage relationship better (write what you can do—not what your mate can do!—like watching your schedule a little more closely, planning weekly one-to-one times, or farming out the kids for an evening):

_____

_____

_____

_____

_____

qualities we desired to have in ours. We loved the way they worked together to improve marriages—beginning with their own. Their vision was bigger than the two of them, and they worked together tirelessly over the years helping other couples like us strengthen our marriages.

We admired their sensitivity to each other. You didn't have to be around them long to know they each had a mind of their own, but they negotiated their differences in a loving way. Their commitment to each other's welfare was obvious as was their commitment to always be open and honest in their communication with each other. They truly enjoyed being together. Just being around them encouraged us.

They taught us much about loving each other and building an enriched healthy marriage. Much of what we do today and share with other couples in our workshops and books (and even in this getaway) is the result of David and Vera's impact on our lives. David passed away several years ago, but through his memory and his writings and our continuing friendship with Vera, the Maces continue to enrich our lives.

Find Marriage Mentors

We hope you will follow our example and look for an older couple who reflect what you desire for your relationship. Actually, your mentors could be a couple your own age or even younger who have the qualities you admire. Discuss other couples you know who might play that role in your life.

Couples whose marriages we admire are:

_____

_____

_____

Now Make it Personal

Picture yourself at the end of this life's race. What qualities would you like your relationship to have? Together write them down:

_____

_____

_____

To fight the good fight and finish the race requires basing your marriage on the right foundation. Do you have a passage of Scripture that is especially meaningful to you when you consider your marriage foundation? If not, choose one now.

A CORD OF THREE STRANDS

A number of years ago we found a passage for our marriage. It is Ecclesiastes 4:9–12:

> Two are better than one,
>   because they have a good return for their work:
> If one falls down,
>   his friend can help him up.
> But pity the man who falls
>   and has no one to help him up!

Also, if two lie down together, they will keep warm.
But how can one keep warm alone?
Though one may be overpowered,
two can defend themselves.
A cord of three strands is not quickly broken. (NIV)

What a beautiful picture of a marriage partnership! It's not a picture of a perfect relationship. It's one where both fall down from time to time, but even in those times, the marriage cord has three strands and holds together. For us that third strand that holds us together when we fall is God, the Holy Spirit. (And personally, we really like the phrase "if two lie down together, they will keep warm!")

What describes your marriage partnership? What would you like to describe it? We challenge you to search Scripture and choose your own verse. We challenge you to consider the godly older couples you know who have true love relationships and choose a mentor couple. Look at your own marriage and choose to grow in intimacy, passion, and commitment to each other. Who knows—one day you may be mentoring marriage for other young couples. We challenge you to build your love relationship today. Then you will be able to pass on a legacy of love to the next generation!

NOW WHAT?

Where do you go from here? We have two suggestions:

1. Choose a time in the next two weeks to talk about and reflect on your marriage getaway experience. Pull out those calendars you brought

and write down when you are going to have your "After-the-Getaway Date."

2. Then turn to the Looking Back and Looking Forward Exercise on pages 93–96. Take a few minutes right now to fill out this exercise. You then have two options. You can discuss it before you leave, or you can save it for the date you just made! Here is one couple's advice: "We would encourage couples not to leave until they fill out the Looking Back and Looking Forward Exercise! It would be too bad to have such a good evaluation/goal planning opportunity get lost in the cracks of the busy modern world which is more demanding when we've been away for a weekend. What worked so well for us was to write out our thoughts before we left for home; then we shared our papers with each other on our follow-up date the next week. It was more meaningful because we both had time to reflect on our getaway and evaluate our goals and plans in the light of reality."

THE END IS THE BEGINNING

You are almost to the end of your getaway, but the end of this weekend is only the beginning of a stronger relationship. We hope that what you have experienced together this weekend will fan the fires of intimacy, passion, and commitment in your love relationship. Hold on to your love. Cherish it, nourish it, protect it, fight for it. Be willing to do what it takes to keep love alive—to build your marriage. Take it from us, it's ultimately worth it!

Looking Back and Looking Forward

Her Copy

Part I: Looking Back

What new insights did we gain?

1. What I learned about you:

_____

_____

_____

2. What I learned about me:

_____

_____

_____

3. What I learned about us:

_____

_____

_____

Part II: Looking Forward

1. What I want for you:

_____

_____

_____

2. What I want for me:

_____

_____

_____

3. What I want for us:

_____
_____
_____

Part III: Setting Goals

Where would we like our marriage to be:

1. In ten years:

_____
_____
_____

2. In one year:

_____
_____
_____

3. In six months:

_____
_____
_____

4. In one month:

_____
_____
_____

Our Action Plan:

_____
_____
_____

Looking Back and Looking Forward
His Copy
Part I: Looking Back

What new insights did we gain?

1. What I learned about you:

_____
_____
_____

2. What I learned about me:

_____
_____
_____

3. What I learned about us:

_____
_____
_____

Part II: Looking Forward

1. What I want for you:

_____
_____
_____

2. What I want for me:

_____
_____
_____

3. What I want for us:

_____
_____
_____

Part III. Setting Goals

Where would we like our marriage to be:

1. In ten years:

_____
_____
_____

2. In one year:

_____
_____
_____

3. In six months:

_____
_____
_____

4. In one month:

_____
_____
_____

Our Action Plan:

_____
_____
_____

PART THREE

GETAWAY ENHANCERS

Chapter Eight

The Ultimate Mini Marriage Builder Menu

Welcome to the Ultimate Mini Marriage Builder Menu. We offer you 52 short, practical exercises. Each Mini Marriage Builder is designed to help you grow and enrich your marriage relationship.

Marriage exercises are like folklore. Many have been passed from couple to couple and we may never know the original source. However, we do want to acknowledge several sources and to recommend their excellent resources to you. We have done this in the last Mini Marriage Builder, Marriage Enrichment Opportunities.

LOOKING AT THE MENU

For your convenience, we've organized the Mini Marriage Builders in four categories: Appetizers, Main Courses, Desserts, and Healthy Snacks.

The Appetizer Exercises are designed to give you an appetite for marriage enrichment, while the Main Courses offer exercises that deal with heavier issues like money matters and spiritual growth.

The most popular Mini Marriage Builders are the Dessert Exercises. Ones such as How Do You Love Each Other? and Granting Three Wishes will help rekindle your flame. Healthy Snacks Exercises are a smorgasbord of topics for you to consider from Taking a Marriage Inventory to The Ultimate Supper Club with a Purpose.

NOTE: The Mini Marriage Builders are not "problem solvers," nor do they give solutions. Instead they provide you the opportunity to come up with your own conclusions.

In some situations, The Mini Marriage Builder will be diagnostic, letting you know you need help. For instance, the "Dealing with Depression" Exercise might get you out of the dumps, but won't cure major depression. However, it could help you find out if you need to seek professional help.

In most cases, each of the Mini Marriage Builders will be a fun, practical catalyst to a meaningful conversation that moves you toward a specific positive action.

What's the Best Approach?

There is no right or wrong way to approach the Mini Marriage Builders. We hope you've already enjoyed several of them during your Getaway Encounter Weekend. In the future, you may want to set a regular time to use them. Be creative. You can randomly choose a topic, or if you like to plan, chart out your agenda.

If you want to design your next getaway around these Mini Marriage Builders, then see Planning Future Getaways on p. 199.

If you enjoy these exercises, you will find more in our book *60 One-Minute Marriage Builders* (Nashville: Thomas Nelson, 1993). Also please refer to other Marriage Enrichment Opportunities on page 201.

We offer the following selections. Our advice is to pick and choose what is appetizing to you! Enjoy!

The Ultimate Mini Marriage Builder Menu

♥ Appetizers ♥

✌ Main Courses ✌

Getaway
Enhancers

The Ultimate
Mini Marriage
Builder
Menu

∽ Healthy Snacks ∾

❧ Appetizers ❧

The Encouragement Exercise

Let us encourage you to build each other up—others will do plenty of tearing down! We need to develop the habit of encouraging each other. Practice complimenting your mate. No one ever gets too much genuine praise. Proverbs 25:11 says, "A word fitly spoken is like apples of gold in settings of silver."

In this Mini Marriage Builder, we want you to concentrate on ways you can sincerely compliment your mate. Make the following lists; then share with each other and talk about how you like to be encouraged!

1. How has your mate encouraged you in the past?

2. How would you like your mate to encourage you in the future?

3. In what areas of life do you feel most competent?

4. Is there an area in which you would like to develop competence (sports, crafts, writing, gourmet cooking, hobbies, education, etc.)?

5. What can you do to encourage your mate to develop competence in a specific area?

Affirm each other today. You're both worth it!

What's Your Marriage Potential?

The Marriage Potential Inventory was developed by Drs. David and Vera Mace early in their work with marriage enrichment.[6] It has been successfully used time and time again to help couples discuss their expectations and assess their relationship.

The best way to approach this exercise is to separately rate your marriage on a scale of 1 to 10 in each of the areas, with 10 representing a very high level of satisfaction and 1 representing low satisfaction. Then come together and talk with your partner about the ratings.

The ten areas are:
1. Common goals and values
2. Commitment to growth
3. Communication skills
4. Creative use of conflict
5. Appreciation or affection
6. Agreement on gender roles
7. Cooperation and teamwork
8. Sexual fulfillment
9. Money management
10. Decision-making

Remember the following points:

• Significant differences in scoring may mean one of two things: differences in expectations or differences in assessment of couple performance.

- A low score in an area by one partner may mean higher expectations in that area.
- The purpose of the exercise is to encourage honest appraisal, promote dialogue, and help you plan for growth in your marriage.

Defining Your Masculinity and Femininity

God in his wisdom created us male and female. In both Matthew 19:4 and Mark 10:6, Jesus reminds us that the Creator made us male and female and created us in God's image. In this context, we are to complement each other and to mirror His image to others. It is a wonderful mystery how this happens, but together, you can be a picture of godly harmony!

Discuss the following questions together:

1. In light of the above, how do you feel about your masculinity or femininity?

2. Define how you express your masculinity or femininity.

3. What threatens your masculinity or femininity?

4. How does our present and past culture affect your attitude toward "maleness" and "femaleness"? (Consider masculine and feminine Hollywood role models—how have they changed over the years? Consider also books like Robert Bly's *Iron John*.)

5. How do you together mirror God's image?

The Discovery Exercise

How much do you know about your mate? Sometimes it's difficult to stay in touch with our partners, and none of us are mind readers! Use the following questions to see how much you know about your mate and what new things you can discover.

You may want to write out your answers and then discuss together, or simply talk through these questions. It's up to you!

1. What has especially pleased your partner during the past month?

2. If you wanted to invite friends to your home for dinner, which two persons (or couple) would your partner choose?

3. If your partner has $100 "free" money, how would he/she want to spend it?

4. What does your partner worry about?

5. For your next getaway weekend as a couple, where might your partner like to go?

6. What are the major pressures your partner is feeling right now?

7. If your partner had a "free day" to spend in any way, what would he/she like to do?

8. Name one specific thing that would make your partner feel special or loved.

Evaluating Your Life-style

While your relationship with each other is very important, your marriage is also influenced by the broader setting in which you live. Your job, community, church, friendship circle, and leisure activities all influence your marriage. Following are several questions to help you look objectively at your life-style. You may want to consider them individually first and then together:

1. List your major interest in life at the present time. What are the things you are really enthusiastic about?

2. Consider your daily working situation. Do you feel you are using the talents God has given you for a good purpose? Do you have the opportunity to express your own creativity? Are your work-related activities satisfying?

3. Are you satisfied with your friendship circle? Do you have individual friends? Are there friends that both of you enjoy? Do you entertain and do fun things with friends as often as you would like? Do you spend time with friends too often?

4. Does the community in which you live provide you with stimulation and opportunities for your enjoyment and personal growth? Do you take advantage of these opportunities? Is this a community where you would like to grow old?

5. Are you satisfied with your church involvement? Do you make a personal contribution of your time and talents? Do you receive spiritual nourishment? Are you growing in your own spiritual pilgrimage?

6. What experiences in the present stimulate your mind and imagination? Are you experiencing personal growth as an individual and as a couple?

7. Are you living a healthy life-style? Do you maintain a healthy diet? Do you exercise regularly? Do you have a hobby?

8. Are there changes in your life-styles you would like to make?

You may want to repeat this exercise in six months!

Separateness and Togetherness

Maybe you're thinking, "I just wish we had more time together." Or maybe you're at the other end of the spectrum; you might be thinking, "We're together too much!" How do you balance your separateness and togetherness in your marriage?

There are lots of things we enjoy doing together, but we also want to keep our own unique identity as persons. To see where you are in this area of togetherness and separateness discuss the following:

List your present activities and responsibilities and divide them into three categories:

A. Things I do alone:

_____

_____

_____

B. Things I do with my mate:

_____

_____

_____

C. Things I do with someone else:

_____

_____

_____

Evaluate your lists. If you do everything alone, that's too much separateness; if you do everything with your mate, it may be too much togetherness.

Now discuss:

1. Are we doing enough creative things together?

2. Are we involved in enough activities to meet our separate needs as individuals?

3. Do we need to make any changes in our activities in order to reach a healthy balance? What is realistic for us at this stage of life?

Now, you may want to pull out your calendars! Take this Mini Marriage Builder seriously. It'll add to the balance sheet of your marriage!

Managing Time Pressures

In our hectic world, when so many couples both work outside the home, managing time has become a critical issue. Following are several questions to help you evaluate how you are dealing with time pressures in your marriage relationship. You may want to go through these questions individually. Then share your findings together and see whether some changes might be desirable.

1. Do I feel in control of my time?

2. Do we each try to avoid overscheduling?

3. Do we each set limits on the time demands of our work?

4. Are we each getting enough sleep to cope effectively during our waking hours?

5. Do we practice punctuality when we have engagements?

6. Do either of us watch television excessively? (You may need to define what "excessive" means to you.)

7. Do we take enough time to keep up with each other's joys, problems, or concerns?

8. Do we make time for our close friends and family members?

9. Do we find time, separately and together, for creative leisure activities?

10. If we have children, do we spend enough time with them?

11. Do we each have some private time for reflection or meditation?

12. What changes would I like to make in how my time is used?

Great Expectations

Do you desire intimacy, closeness, and the deep sharing of life's experiences with your mate? Sharing life deeply with one another and being loved, trusted, and appreciated even in light of our weaknesses gives us a sense of identity and self-confidence in our marriage relationship.

Let's look at seven areas of expectations in marriage. As you read through the list, rank these expectations in order of their importance to you (1 for very important; 7 for unimportant). Then go back through the list and rank them according to their importance to your mate.

Share your rankings with each other. Then look back at the list and circle the expectations that may not have been met. Think about these expectations as you set goals for your marriage.

Getaway
Enhancers

Wife *Husband*

___ ___ 1. Security—The knowledge of permanence in the relationship and of financial and material well-being

___ ___ 2. Companionship—Having a friend who goes through all the joys and sorrows of life with you, a soul partner; having common areas of interest

___ ___ 3. Sex—The oneness that comes through physical intimacy in marriage; the initiation and enjoyment of a growing physical relationship

___ ___ 4. Understanding and tenderness—Experiencing regularly the touch, the kiss, the wink across the room that says, "I love you," "I care," "I'm thinking of you"

___ ___ 5. Encouragement—Having someone verbally support and appreciate your work and efforts in your profession, in your home, with the children, and so on

___ ___ 6. Intellectual closeness—Discussing and growing together in common areas of intellectual thought

___ ___ 7. Mutual activity—Doing things together—in politics, sports, church work, hobbies, etc.

Middle Age Marriage

This exercise is for couples who are in the middle years of life and have been married for a number of years. It's always good to stop and evaluate your marriage, but it is especially helpful at this stage of life. Together discuss the following questions:

1. Over the years as you have grown together, what are your best memories? Do you have them cataloged through pictures, scrapbooks, slides, and/or videos?

2. What has been the most difficult "new horizon" in your relationship?

3. In what ways has your marriage "grown up"?

4. What "new horizons" do you see in your future?

5. Are there things you have to give up or let go of as you move through the middle years together?

6. How has your role as parents affected your relationship as partners?

7. What do you enjoy (or look forward to) about the empty nest?

8. Is there a dream you have had on the back burner for years that you can now revive and fulfill?

9. Are you both satisfied with the way in which you use your discretionary time, both separately and together?

10. Have you planned for your retirement years? (If not, perhaps this is a good time to begin to talk about it.)

Reading Together

How long has it been since you have read together? To read a book or article and then discuss it with each other is one way of growing together intellectually. A whole new area of intimacy in marriage can emerge when we start sharing thoughts and feelings generated by good literature. Here are some suggestions to get you started:

1. Try reading a book out loud together. (You may have gotten experience doing this during your getaway weekend!) It's a great way to relax together, perhaps at night when you go to bed. (One couple we know, who have been married over fifty years, told us that the wife reads jokes from the *Reader's Digest* to her husband each evening before they go to sleep!)

2. Read the same book privately. Let one of you underline things of interest in red and the other in blue. Then choose a time to have your own "Book Date" and talk about it, using these questions:

- What is being said?
- How is it being said?
- What is the author's goal?
- Where do I stand on this issue?

3. Ask what your mate is already reading. Then read it and discuss.

4. Save interesting magazine and newspaper articles and share them with each other.

Leisure and Recreation in Marriage

The heart of the word *recreation* is *re-create*. There are times in marriage we need to find relaxation, renewal, and in a sense be put together again in a new and more exciting way. Recreation and leisure cover a very wide field. They include things we do together as well as things we enjoy doing individually.

Take a look at the kinds of ways in which you seek relaxation and renewal. You may want to begin by separately making your individual lists; and then get together to see how your individual choices can be shared and in what situations you can manage better separately. Consider these categories:

1. Athletic activities I enjoy alone:

2. Athletic activities we enjoy as a couple:

3. Athletic activities we enjoy with others:

4. Social interaction (visiting, games, competitions, etc.):

5. Reading (together or alone):

6. Home entertainment (television, videos, music, radio):

7. Outside entertainment (movies, concerts, lectures, sports, etc.):

8. Travel:

Now share your lists with each other and categorize in the following way:

1. We prefer to do these things alone and separately:

2. We enjoy doing these things together:

3. We like to do these things with a group of friends:

Ask yourselves: Are we both getting the recreation we need to stay healthy, happy, and well-balanced? If not, what changes do we need to make?

Rut Busters

Our culture today doesn't encourage fun and adventure in marriage. We get married, and then we "settle down." How boring! What can you do to stir up fun and excitement in your marriage? We suggest busting out of your ruts!

Make a list of out-of-character, fun things you would like to do with your mate. Consult *52 Dates for You and Your Mate* for ideas. Here are some suggestions we got from spouses of publishers. Add your own.

1. Go to a really nice hotel. Walk through the grounds and lobby and enjoy the ambience. Have an intimate conversation and dinner or dessert if you like.

2. Put on your nicest pajamas, play soft music, light candles, and enjoy an intimate dinner for two—right in your own home.

3. Take a spur-of-the-moment trip together.

4. Buy a double rocker or swing for your porch.

5. Sleep out on your balcony or screen porch.

6. Read aloud together.

7. For empty-nesters, borrow small children and go to the zoo.

8. Ride a bike built for two.

9. Go for a walk in the rain.

10. Buy season tickets to the symphony (or whatever you both enjoy)!

❧ Main Courses ❧

Taking a Marriage Checkup

We take regular health checkups and dental checkups, why not a marriage checkup? You get a checkup when there are no big problems, and by doing so often you avoid problems down the road. Here's our suggestion: take time to discuss and evaluate the following four questions:

1. What are the resources on which we can draw at the present time for the nurturing of our relationship (things like health, mutual faith in God, praying together, steady work, etc.)?

2. What particular qualities and gifts do I personally have to invest in our marriage at the present time?

3. If someone looked at our marriage, what would he or she say were our present priorities? Are they in the right order?

4. Is there anything that I am withholding that I could and should be giving to our marriage at the present time? energy? concentration? practical help? loving support? If I am withholding anything, why am I doing so?

Now summarize what you have talked about and write out your prescription for marital health.

Daily Sharing Times

From our friends, David and Vera Mace, comes the suggestion to honor your marriage commitment by having a daily sharing time. It will keep you daily communicating with each other and only takes ten minutes. (Of course, it can be extended when you want!)

The Maces suggest having your sharing time at a regular time each day. For them the best time was the first thing in the morning over a cup of tea.

To have your own daily sharing time, claim your ten minutes and talk about these three questions:

1. How are you feeling now about what has happened to you since our last sharing time?

2. What plans do you have for the next twenty-four hours, and is anything troubling you?

3. Are you aware of any issue in our relationship about which we need to talk together in depth; and if so, can we now schedule a time when we will do so?

Your sharing time questions may vary, but what matters is to keep in touch with each other about experiences that affect your relationships but might not be shared unless you create a plan for doing so. Why not take the Maces' suggestion and try a sharing time for the next month? You just may make a new habit!

Growing Together Spiritually

This exercise can help you and your spouse consider the role faith plays in your life individually and as a couple. After discussing these questions together, you may gain a greater understanding and appreciation of why God called the two of you together and what you can do to more effectively minister with and to each other.[7]

1. In what ways are you working *individually* to develop a deeper faith and Christian spirituality (such as attending and participating in church activities, reading the Bible and praying, participating in a Bible study group, giving to charitable causes, helping others)?

2. In what ways are you working *together* as a couple to develop a deeper faith and Christian spirituality (such as praying together, studying the Bible together, attending church)?

3. Are you and your spouse satisfied with your church? If not, what is the cause of your dissatisfaction?

4. Are you satisfied with your current level of church involvement?

5. Do you feel you are devoting too little time, too much time, or the right amount of time to individual ministry projects (like serving on church committees, teaching Sunday school)?

6. Do you feel that you or your spouse or the two of you together

are devoting too little time, too much time, or the right amount of time to your shared ministry projects?

7. What kind of support do you need from your spouse to nurture your own spirituality?

8. What can you do to support your spouse in meeting his/her spiritual needs?

9. What can you do to serve as an example to your spouse to encourage his/her further spiritual development?

Talking about Money

One point of contention in many marriages is money. Some couples have a hard time even talking about it. The following exercise is designed to help you talk and better understand how both of you look at this touchy subject.

1. If you received $10,000 tax free, what would you do with it?

2. Do you agree or disagree with the following statements: Put an A (agree) or D (disagree) by each statement. Then discuss.

_____ I'm basically too tight with money.

_____ My mate is basically too tight with money.

_____ Making financial decisions together is important to me.

_____ I'm comfortable with the way we make financial decisions.

_____ Sometimes I buy things I don't need just because they're on sale.

_____ I really like to give to good causes like my church, Christian organizations, community organizations, and people in need.

_____ I really like to use credit cards.

_____ I hate credit cards with a passion.

_____ I always balance my checkbook.

_____ I feel uncomfortable borrowing money.

_____ I believe in enjoying today and letting tomorrow worry about itself.

_____ A regular savings plan is important to me.

3. What was the most sensible thing we have done with money since we were married?

The most foolish?

4. What money issues are the most frequent causes of disagreement?

5. How satisfied are you with the division of responsibility between the two of you in handling money matters?

Four Styles of Communication

There are four styles of communication that we all use from time to time. Some are helpful and others are not. See if you identify with these:

Style One: Chitchat—Chitchat refers to surface conversations. These "Hi, how are you's?" are part of healthy communication. The problem arises when all we ever do is chitchat. It's safe, but it's shallow.

Style Two: Attacking—Attacking is the communication style that hurts! We attack the other person without even thinking about what we're doing. Clues that you are in Style Two communication are "You" statements and "Why" questions. The goal when we find ourselves attacking is to stop it. Choose a signal that lets your partner know he or she is treading on thin ice. We simply say, "Ouch, I feel a pinch!" A signal lets your spouse know that whether it was intended or not, you felt attacked.

Style Three: Problem Solving—This is the style of communication we want to use so that we can resolve whatever issue we are dealing with. Logical, problem-solving communication takes place when you write down the problems, brainstorm possible solutions, and then choose the one that seems most appropriate and give it a try. The problem is that if we have been in Style Two and our emotions are stirred up, it's hard if not impossible to suddenly become logical and solve the problem. That's why we need the fourth style of communication.

Style Four: Expressing Feelings—This is the working style of communication in any healthy marriage. First, you need to agree that you don't want to be in attack mode and that together you will attack the problem, not each other. Focus on the problem and simply state how you feel about it. For instance, "Let me tell you how I feel. I feel hurt, angry, frustrated, anxious." (Add whatever describes how you really feel.)

Now ask your partner for feedback. "Tell me how you feel about this issue." Then really listen.

Soon you both will have calmed down enough to go on and solve the problem. (If you want more help in learning to communicate on a feelings level, consult chapter 4, Communicating Our Feelings, in our book *The Marriage Track*. It contains several exercises you may find helpful.)

1. Now together talk about the four styles of communication. Make a commitment to each other to identify attacking whenever you find yourself using it. Come up with a signal that will help you!

2. Make a list of feeling words that you could use to communicate.

3. Practice telling each other how you feel about various things. (See the next Mini Marriage Builder for a list of subjects to talk about.)

"How Do I Feel When..."

As a couple, it is important to share feelings with each other. If you have not been in the habit of sharing your feelings, the following exercise will give you the opportunity to practice. Reflect on the following situations. Then share your feelings with each other, taking turns in answering first.

How do I feel when:

1. You surprise me with something nice?
2. You show that you appreciate me?
3. I make a mistake and you point it out?
4. You are holding me tight?
5. You give me a compliment?
6. I think that you are judging me?
7. You make a sacrifice for me?
8. Others notice how close we are?
9. You tell me you love me?
10. You appear to be annoyed with me?
11. I am buying a gift for you?
12. I can't make you understand?
13. You frown at me?
14. You are too hard on yourself?
15. You are too hard on me?
16. You smile at me?
17. You reach out and touch me?

18. You interrupt me?
19. I think I have hurt your feelings?
20. You are upset and begin to cry?
21. You are sick?
22. You ask me to help you?
23. You make me laugh?
24. You become angry with me?
25. You tell me you are proud of me?

Please refer to the Mini Marriage Builder Four Styles of Communication, page 137, for help in sharing feelings in a positive way.

Family Planning

While our plans don't always work out just the way we want them to, it is still important to plan. And one big area for partners is family planning. Following are questions you may want to discuss if you are still at the family-planning age.

1. How many children would I like to have?

2. What would be the ideal spacing of children?

3. How do I feel about birth control? Am I happy with our present situation?

4. How do I feel about adoption? Would I ever be open to adopting?

5. What are my favorite names for a girl? for a boy? Do I want to use family names?

6. How do I feel about child care?

7. What educational goals do I desire for our children?

8. Do I feel ready to start our family?

Becoming Close Companions

Are you best friends in your marriage? Are you a good companion to your mate? The following questions from David and Vera Mace will help you answer these questions and identify ways you can be close companions.

These questions will explore the quality of your marriage at the companionship level. Either consider them separately and then come together to share your findings, or spontaneously talk them over together.

You may want to go beyond a yes or no answer. You can use the question our Marriage Encounter friends use. Follow each question's answer with HDIFAT (How do I feel about that?).

1. Do I behave toward you as though you were a very important (even the most important) person in my life?

2. When I am with you in the presence of others, do I act toward you in ways that communicate to others that our relationship is one of close companionship?

3. Do I sense your needs and try to meet them in ways that make you feel understood and loved?

4. Do I recognize clearly and try to understand differences in the ways we have learned to behave as a result of our family backgrounds and our earlier life experiences?

5. Do we spend enough time alone together to meet each other's needs for intimacy and sharing?

6. Do we take enough time to do enjoyable things together?

7. Do we have enough flexibility to change our behavior patterns and to try new ways of responding to each other?

8. Do I give you enough encouragement and affirmation to make you feel supported in our relationship?

9. When I challenge you, do I manage to do it without nagging or putting you down?

10. Do I generally behave toward you in ways that make you feel good about yourself?

Parenting

One of the most awesome challenges in life is parenting our children. Sometimes it is overwhelming, but it's much easier and more pleasant when we parent as partners and when we are united in our parenting philosophy. Discuss the following questions to help you evaluate where you are in your parenting role.[8]

1. What is the basis of a strong family? (You may want to read together Psalm 127.)

2. Where are we right now in our relationship with each child? (You may actually want to write down, in twenty-five words or less, a description of your present relationship with each child.)

3. Where would we like to be? (In twenty-five words or less, describe what your ideal relationship with each child would be. Write separate statements for each child.)

4. What areas need improvement?

5. What changes do we need to make to better parent as partners?

Learning to Negotiate

How do you handle conflict? Do you identify with any of our animal friends:

- The Turtle—the withdrawer
- The Skunk—the fighter
- The Gorilla—the winner
- The Chameleon—the yielder
- The Owl—the intellectualizer
- The Beaver—the avoider

If both of you agreed on everything, one of you would be unnecessary. Life involves negotiating, and nowhere is negotiating more needed than in a marriage relationship. What is causing tension in your relationship at the present time? Together make a list of areas of conflict in your marriage. Many times it's the little things that cause tension, like who gets the remote control, who returns calls from the answering machine, or who leaves the top off the toothpaste, as well as the major matters like money, children, priorities, and time management. (For more on learning to negotiate, see chapter 9, "Getting Back on When You Jump Track," in our book *The Marriage Track*.)

To learn how to negotiate, choose one issue, preferably the least emotional one, and talk through these four steps:

Step 1: Define the problem.
It may help to actually write out whatever it is you are trying to resolve. The problem is:

_____

Step 2: Identify specific factors contributing to the problem.

_____

_____

_____

Step 3: List alternative solutions.
Actually write out possible solutions. It helps if you have a sense of humor and a wild imagination.

_____

_____

_____

Step 4: Select a plan of action.
Choose one possible solution from Step 3 and give it a try. If it doesn't work, try another. Together focus on the problem. This way you can attack the problem and not each other—you may even resolve it! **Our plan of action is**

_____

_____

_____

Learning to Process Anger

Marriage specialists David and Vera Mace say that the biggest problem in marriage is not the lack of communication but the inability to handle and process anger.[9] They remind us that anger is a normal, healthy emotion. A person who doesn't get angry is not a normal human being. However, once angry, we are responsible for what we do about it. Venting anger simply increases the intensity. Suppressing anger is also unhealthy. The Maces suggest that a better way to handle anger is to process it, and they developed a three-step system for doing just that.

They made a contract with each other that they would help each other put it into operation at the first sign of anger. Here are their three steps:

Step 1: We agree to acknowledge our anger to each other as soon as we become aware of it.

Step 2: We renounce the right to vent anger at each other. It's OK to say something like, "I'm getting angry with you, but you know I'm not going to attack you." The other person does not have to go on the defensive.

Step 3: We each ask for the other's help in dealing with anger that develops. If your partner is angry with you and appeals to you to help clear it up, it is very much in your interest to respond. The Maces suggest forming a coalition. They say, "Our contract commits us to working on each anger situation that develops between us until we clear it up."

Now talk about how you handle anger—or would like to handle anger—in your marriage relationship. Discuss the Maces' three-step system. If you want to make a similar contract with each other, here is your opportunity.

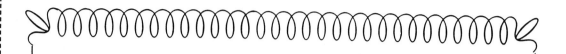

Whenever One of Us Becomes Angry

1. We will acknowledge our anger to each other as soon as we become aware of it.

2. We will renounce the right to vent anger at each other.

3. We will ask for each other's help in dealing with the anger that has developed.

Signed _____

Signed _____

Developing a Couple Prayer Life

Praying together as a couple can bring unity and intimacy in a unique way. As you commit your lives and concerns to your heavenly Father, it's easier to focus and achieve a real sense of oneness. Praying together will help you to discern God's direction for your future.

We suggest setting aside a specific time to pray together.[10] One couple we know prays together each morning before they get out of bed. Another couple has their prayer time each evening before bedtime. From time to time, we have taken a whole day or a half day to concentrate on prayer. Our prayer time is not very structured, but we suggest the following:

1. Read Scripture together
2. Talk about how God has led you in the past
3. Share answered prayers you have observed
4. Write down specific prayer requests
5. Make a list of things you want to pray for each other and for each of your children (and others who are close to you) for the next year. (You may want to make duplicate lists to tuck in each of your Bibles.)
6. Most importantly, actually pray together!

Try having a Prayer Date. You will find you feel more connected to each other and to God after such a date. This is especially appropriate when you are making a transition such as a job change or move or entering a new stage of family life, like the empty nest.

Choosing Chores

One area of common stress in marriage is completing all the chores. "Isn't it time somebody took out the garbage?"[11] is more than a trite question. This exercise will help you divvy up household chores, cut down on disagreements, and free up more time for doing the things you enjoy.

When deciding who will do what, it's helpful to consider how often each task needs to be performed. Meal preparation is daily but income tax returns are filed yearly. To complete this exercise, note the frequency of each task and then mark the person responsible for each task. (In some cases, the solution may involve recruiting your kids or outside help.)

TASKS	Frequency	Husband	Wife	Other
Laundry				
Ironing				
Dishes				
Prepares breakfast				
Prepares (or packs) lunches				
Prepares dinner				
Cares for the pet(s)				
Dusts				
Makes the beds				
Sweeps, vacuums the floors				

TASKS	Frequency	Husband	Wife	Other
Cleans the bathroom				
Takes care of household repairs				
Cleans out the closet				
Cleans out the garage				
Cleans out the basement				
Cleans out the refrigerator				
Coordinates family calendar				
Sends out greeting cards				
Maintains medical records				
Balances the checkbook				
Pays the bills				
Keeps financial records				
Prepares income tax returns				
Carries trash out to the curb				
Walks the dog				
Takes care of the dry cleaning				
Buys groceries				
Returns library books/rented videos				
Washes windows				
Takes care of the lawn				
Tends the garden				
Rakes leaves				
Shovels snow				
Prunes trees, trims hedges				

Getaway
Enhancers

TASKS	Frequency	Husband	Wife	Other
Takes care of auto repairs and maintenance				
Cleans out the rain gutters				
Paints the house				
Takes the kids to school and other activities				
Takes the kids to the doctor				
Attends parent/teacher conferences				
Buys clothes for the kids				
Does the banking				

Long-term Planning—Setting Marriage Goals

Where do you want your marriage relationship to be in five years? ten years? twenty-five years? What do you want your marriage to look like on your fiftieth wedding anniversary?

To answer these questions, we suggest that you set some marriage goals and based on those goals do some long range planning. Following is a list of possible marriage goals. Use this list as a catalyst to come up with your own long-term goals and plans.

Marriage Goals:

1. To develop a deeper personal relationship with my mate; to develop common interests and get to know my mate better

2. To improve communication with my mate and to learn to express myself better

3. To improve and become more creative in our sexual relationship

4. To become more united and responsible in our finances

5. To learn to resolve conflict and process anger in a positive way that builds our relationship instead of tear it down

6. To work on a common project together or learn something together or complete a service project for someone else

7. To develop a vision for making a difference in our community and world

Now take a sheet of paper and list your own marriage goals.

Our marriage goals are:

Choose the first area you want to begin to work on and answer these three questions:

1. What? (Write down your long-term goal.)

2. How? (Outline your short-term plan. It should be realistic and measurable so you will know if you are making progress.)

3. When? (This question is the nitty-gritty; fill in on your calendar what you are committing yourself to do!)

Now make a commitment to each other to follow through with your plans. From time to time evaluate how you are doing and focus on different goals.

For more help in setting marriage goals, see chapter 6, Setting Goals for Your Marriage, in our book *The Marriage Track*.

Evaluating Your Attitude Toward Finances

Are finances a sensitive subject in your relationship? Money and the handling of it is a sore spot with many couples. Often we come into marriage with different viewpoints and styles of managing money. Whether you have little or much, the key issues are communicating about finances and pulling together for solutions instead of pushing apart.

To see if you are united in this area, discuss the following three questions:

1. Have you had a disagreement or felt tension in your relationship caused by finances in the last month? If so, what was the issue? How did you resolve it? Were you both happy with the solution?

2. What part do you think your individual backgrounds play? (Maybe one of you grew up in a very frugal home and the other grew up thinking money grew on trees.)

3. What happens when money is really tight? When you are under financial pressure, do you place blame or do you pull together? What would you like to be able to do?

Now look at your own financial situation and discuss what changes you would like to make.

Taming Perfection

Has anyone ever accused you of being a perfectionist? Have you ever accused anyone, especially your spouse, of being a perfectionist? And if you have ever accused or been accused, what's the big deal? Isn't it good to be disciplined, organized, physically fit—perfect? In theory, yes. In practice, none of us can ever achieve perfection. And it is this desire to be perfect, when carried to extreme, that characterizes a perfectionist.

Perfectionism is often something that has developed over a person's lifetime. A child never quite meets his parents' expectations and so he continues to strive for approval and perfection as an adult. Or a child may have gone without many luxuries or conveniences and so she now sets a higher standard for herself—perfection. Certainly there is not enough time to explore the intricacies of perfectionism here in this builder. If perfectionism exists in your marriage, is it taking a negative toll on your relationship? If so, there are things you can do to overcome this cycle of perfectionism. First, answer these questions.

1. Do you see some signs of perfectionism in yourself? Your mate?

2. How does your or your spouse's perfectionism show up in your life and your marriage? (For example: *I cannot go to bed unless the house is clean. I get mad when someone has moved things around on my desk—even if it is just a little bit. I am often frustrated when my spouse doesn't set the same standards I do.*)

3. Does perfectionism taint your family relationships, especially with your children? (Remember, this is an opportunity for the two of you to

recognize a dynamic in your lives for the purpose of improving your marriage and your family, not a time for accusation.)

4. What are the ways in which high standards have benefited your relationship? (For example: *I do stick to my exercise program now, thanks to my spouse's prodding. I am so proud of the way the house looks when guests come over, and it is all due to my spouse's hard work.*)

Now, after acknowledging that perfectionism has its benefits and pitfalls, discuss the areas in which perfectionism has taken such a toll that change is essential.

As we said before, there are steps you can take to overcome your cycle of perfectionism. Just acknowledging that this is a problem is a step in the right direction. But take this discussion a few steps further. Together, commit to change this perfectionistic behavior. Of course, the person with the perfectionistic behaviors needs to initiate this commitment, but a spouse can be an excellent source of feedback and accountability. Write out your commitment noting the specific area you will focus on. (It is not necessary to address every area at once—just pick one.)

Now spend some time either together or apart imagining what a less-than-perfect result would be. Discuss together how you can encourage this less-than-perfect goal.

Finally realize that this exercise is just a start. Changing the behaviors of perfectionism is a difficult but rewarding task. Remember that overcoming perfectionism does not mean relinquishing all of your standards. It does mean reevaluating your standards and allowing yourself and others to fall short of the mark without losing respect. This process will involve understanding and flexibility from both of you. We recommend that you read the book *Hope for the Perfectionist* by Dr. David Stoop (Nashville: Thomas Nelson, 1987). Dr. Stoop's book can facilitate changes in behavior and help you determine if professional help is needed in your situation.

Dealing with Depression

Everyone gets the blues now and then. Maybe you had a bad day at work and feel like staying in bed and crying for a week, but instead you take a nap, watch a sad movie, and get on with life. There are some people, however, who have a harder time getting over depression. They may actually stay in bed for a week, or month, without ever feeling better. Sometimes a person is so depressed that they show no emotion whatsoever—they just exist.

Periodic bouts with the blues are normal for everyone. We couldn't stay happy all the time! And we all know the value of watching a sad movie every now and then. But for those people whose depression is lasting, this can take a serious toll on their mental health and on their marriage. How can you tell if you are seriously depressed, or how about your mate? Major depression is characterized by symptoms such as:

- poor appetite
- insomnia
- decreased sex drive
- fatigue
- feelings of worthlessness or guilt
- inability to concentrate
- thoughts of death or suicide

Do you or your spouse have two or more of the symptoms listed above?

Can you identify life circumstances that may have influenced your or your spouse's depressed feelings?

How has this depression affected your relationship? (For example: *I don't feel supported anymore because my spouse is so consumed by his own sadness. We both experienced the loss of a loved one and can't bear each other's burdens now—we feel so alone.*)

Commit to seek support. List friends and relatives you can call on when you need to feel some extra support. Discuss professional counselling and its merits for one or both of you.

Identify ways in which you can support each other until you receive professional or support group assistance.

NOTE: The purpose of this builder is not to diagnose yourself with major depression, but rather to find out if you need to seek some professional help and to determine how you, as a couple, can address this problem.

Sometimes life circumstances can cause depression. The death of a loved one, loss of a job, even a move can result in feelings of sadness and depression. If this is your situation, consider joining a support group for people who have shared your particular trauma. Even seeking professional one-on-one or marriage counselling can give you insight into your grief and can help you overcome your negative feelings.

If there is nothing specific that you can identify as a source of your depression, yet you still have several of the above mentioned symptoms, you should seek professional help. Unexplained depression can last indefinitely and can be the result of unacknowledged childhood trauma, or an unacknowledged conflict in your marriage, or it can even be the result of a chemical imbalance in your brain.

❧ Desserts ❧

How Do You Love Each Other?

If marriage is primarily a love relationship, are you willing to talk together about how you love each other now?[12] If so, here are some questions to consider together:

1. Take turns in describing how, in the early days, each of you fell in love with the other.

2. What qualities in your spouse did you most admire before you decided to marry?

3. In your first year together, what were the qualities in your spouse that sustained romantic love?

4. In the development of companionship love, what qualities in both of you united you into a permanent relationship?

5. How would you define your love for each other now in terms of romance, intimacy, and companionship?

6. Are there any areas on which you need to work further?

Improving Your
Sexual Relationship

If lovemaking has become a dull routine or if you can't seem to find the time or energy, discussing the following questions may help revive the vitality.[13] Just as important as expressing your feelings is really listening to those of your mate! Discuss together the following questions.

1. Does the word *sex* produce positive or negative feelings in you? Why? If you're ambivalent (sometimes you feel positive and sometimes negative), can you identify the specific times and reasons? Maybe this word produces no feelings; if this is the case, can you identify the reason for your numbness?

2. How would you describe the ideal love relationship? Be specific.

3. Has sex with your spouse become a routine act for you, or is it a true expression of shared love? Why or why not?

4. Aside from the sexual act, how do you feel about your sexuality—your masculinity, your femininity? In this area, where do you need the most affirmation?

5. Do you trust your spouse in sexual areas? Why or why not? Do you see this as your problem, your spouse's problem, or a combination?

6. What do you see as the major hindrance in the sexual part of your marriage?

7. In your love relationship with your spouse, what communicates true intimacy?

8. What could you do differently to enhance your love relationship to renew the spark?

Granting Three Wishes

One wife met her husband at the door one evening with a quiver and three arrows with hearts. "Tonight is your night! I'm your fairy godmother, and I will grant you three wishes!"

This particular fairy godmother was quite vague about what happened next, but the giggle and silly look on her face told us it was fun and romantic. While not asking specific details, we did gather some practical suggestions just in case you feel like turning into a fairy godmother or fairy godfather.

First, this warning: you've got to be in the mood. One more caution: some people may find that granting three unqualified wishes is a little too threatening. What if a mate asked you to do something that you don't want to do or is distasteful to you?

If worries like these run through your mind, you can beforehand make a list of acceptable wishes (together or separately). Then you can relax and enjoy bringing pleasure to your mate.[14]

A few wish suggestions are:

• Thirty-minute back rub

• Foot massage and pedicure

• Bathing your mate (gently, the way you would bathe a baby)

• Take a shower together and wash each other's hair

Now list your ideas.

This can be the beginning of your own brand of creativity. At any rate it should add some sparkle to your love life!

Learning to Talk about the "S" Word

Sometimes it is difficult to talk about the most intimate part of the marriage relationship. If you are hesitant to say how you really feel about your sexual relationship, this exercise will help you to begin to talk to each other.

We suggest that you simply read the questions and write down the number of each question on a blank piece of paper; then respond with OK if all is well or with a question mark if some discussion would be helpful. Then, share your responses with each other and take it from there.

1. Do you let your mate know when a sexual experience has been especially enjoyable?

2. Does your mate let you know when he/she is especially enjoying your sex relationship?

3. Do you let your mate know what turns you off sexually?

4. Do you let your mate know what turns you on sexually?

5. Are you open to suggestions from your mate for improving your sex life? If not, are you willing to talk about it?

6. Do you both agree about the frequency of lovemaking?

7. Does your mate understand your sexual needs?

8. Do you feel you understand the sexual needs of your mate?

9. Can you discuss freely together all aspects of your sexual relationship with each other?

10. Are you physically affectionate with each other?

11. Do both of you find it easy to ask the other to make love?

The Bible on Sex

Growing up, did you get the impression that sex is sinful?

Certainly the Bible teaches that God intended the sexual union to be experienced within the framework of marriage. But Scripture teaches that God created sex for our enjoyment and pleasure as well as for procreation. Think about it. Only the man needs to reach orgasm in order for the couple to have children, but God also created woman with the capability of responding with orgasm in the sexual union. Many people overlook the fact that sex was God's idea.

The Bible discusses sex openly and matter-of-factly, acknowledging that it is a precious gift from God. Consider Proverbs 5:18–19: "Let your fountain be blessed, / And rejoice in the wife of your youth. / As a loving hind and a graceful doe, / Let her breasts satisfy you at all times; / Be exhilarated always with her love" (NASB).

Look again at Genesis 2:24–25: "For this cause a man shall leave his father and his mother, and shall cleave to his wife; and they shall become one flesh. And the man and his wife were both naked and were not ashamed" (NASB).

God put His stamp of approval on the sexual union in marriage. He not only approves of it, He invented it! It is to be an expression of love between husband and wife, fulfilling and enjoyable.

Take some time to review the Scriptures we have mentioned here and discuss your thoughts and feelings about God's perspective on sex.[15] ❧

What Now, My Love?

When thinking about mentors for our marriage, we have added a new couple, Dave and Jeanie Stanley. We had the delightful experience of meeting them recently when we were the keynote speakers at the United Marriage Encounter International Celebration, and the Stanleys were our personal hosts. From the time they picked us up at the airport, we could see that this couple—married over forty-five years—had a special spark of love for each other.

Our curiosity got the best of us, so one afternoon when we were not giving a presentation, we attended their workshop entitled, "What Now, My Love?" They shared with us how they keep playfulness and fun in their marriage, and it is with their permission that we share some of their jewels with you.

The basis of the joy in their marriage is their relationship with God. They start their day with wake-up prayer as they snuggle in bed. They like to pray when they are walking and often kneel in prayer together. Along with prayer, they read Scripture together and share their feelings with each other. This practice provides the foundation for the fun and fascinating ideas they shared. You're going to love these!

1. They have pet names for each other—not just two or three. They have hundreds and seem to add more daily! One of their pet names is "Lover Bunnies." There's a reason; they love rabbits and have four (the stuffed variety) who always travel with them.

2. They admitted openly that they are in their second childhood or have never left the first one!

3. They continually look for ways to give each other compliments. "As plants need water," they shared, "we need affirmation from each other."

4. They write each other love letters.

5. They may be older, but their romance and physical affection have just gotten better. Romance depends on your attitude and perspective, they say. And they've kept the right perspective by creating special kisses such as their "clap kiss." "What might be considered sexual harassment at work can bring enjoyment and pleasure at home!" they add.

6. They plan regular dates. (A couple after our own heart!)

7. They handle conflict with a light touch. They have a ten-minute silence rule. At any time, either can call for ten minutes of silence. (If nonverbal communication is a problem, they also have an out of sight for ten minutes rule.) This helps them to calm down and get things back in perspective.

8. They read the Song of Solomon to each other.

9. At airports, they fake good-bye kisses and then get on the plane together.

10. At grocery store checkout counters, Dave asks Jeanie to marry him all over again! Jeanie enthusiastically says "Yes!"

11. They affectionately tease each other, but they are never unkind and they avoid vulnerable spots.

12. They look for things to laugh about.

13. They have shared goals that are bigger than they are. Together they have committed themselves to three big causes; one goal is to strengthen marriages through the ministry of United Marriage Encounter.

Jeanie and Dave, we salute you and thank you for being role models for us and many other couples. The next exercise is composed of questions Dave and Jeanie developed to help couples put more fun in their marriages.

Romancing Your Mate

Dave and Jeanie Stanley are romantics. They are also fun people. And they believe every couple can add more fun and romance to their marriage relationship. The Stanleys have developed a number of discussion questions to help you do just that, and they shared them in their workshop at the United Marriage Encounter International Celebration. It is with their permission that we pass them on to you.

You may want to write down your responses to the questions and then talk about them. Or you can simply talk through the questions together, taking turns going first. However you approach it, it's going to make you think!

1. How can we bring more laughter and good humor into our marriage?

2. What pet names do you call me that I really like? Are there some names that I don't like?

3. Do we tease each other affectionately or hurtfully?

4. What kinds of affectionate touches do I especially like?

5. How and when do we show affection for each other in public?

6. What compliment(s) have you given me recently that I especially appreciated? What were my feelings when you gave me that compliment?

7. What kinds of dates would I like to have with you? When can we schedule them?

8. What are we living for that is bigger than we are?

9. How could our marriage be more Christ-centered?

10. How could we improve our couple prayer life?

11. Is our church involvement bringing us closer or dividing us? What changes would I like to see in our church involvement?

12. What should be the mission statement of our marriage?

13. How do I see us spending our lives after our children leave home?

14. How do I see us spending our lives after retirement?

15. What can we do today just for fun and romance?

From Good Sex to Great Sex

Consider your experience with sex education, formal and/or informal. What are your first memories of talking about sex?

Whether our parents used the *S* word or not, our being here is evidence that our parents had at least some interest in sex. Is that hard to believe? Probably all kids at some time are convinced that their parents really don't have sex! It's especially hard for teenagers to think about their parents as sexual creatures. What do you remember from your home? You may want to check the following statements that describe your childhood environment:

_____ My parents never or rarely used the *S* word.

_____ My parents openly talked about sex in a way that made it seem natural and positive.

_____ My parents rarely showed physical affection for each other or with me.

_____ I come from a family of huggers. My parents were very affectionate with each other and with me.

_____ I was uncomfortable asking my parents about sexual things. I basically learned about the specifics of sex from other sources.

_____ I was comfortable asking my parents about sexual things. They were my major source of sex education.

_____ I received mixed messages about sex. I wasn't sure if it was good or bad.

_____ Based on my parents' attitudes, I looked forward to having a sexual relationship in marriage someday.

Now evaluate what types of statements you checked from the above list. If your parents were comfortable with the word *sex,* and were open and honest and positive about sex with you, count yourself among the very fortunate. If, more typically, your parents choked on the word *sex* and left many questions unanswered, you may have entered marriage with a confused picture of sex. Discussing your "sex education" is one way to open up communication with your mate in this most important area.

Now think about what puts you in a loving mood. What about your mate? You may want to stop and talk about it right now.

Loving Mood Instigators

The things that tend to put me in a loving mood are:

The things that I think put my mate in a loving mood are:

Taking the SAT
(Sexual Attitude Test)

Check the following statements that apply to you. Give yourself one point for each statement checked.

_____ I enjoy my sexual relationship with my mate.

_____ I think he or she enjoys it too.

_____ I look forward to the next time of physical intimacy.

_____ My mate tells me that he or she is satisfied with our sexual relationship.

_____ I am satisfied with our sexual relationship.

_____ I initiate lovemaking from time to time.

_____ I plan special times for us to be alone together.

_____ We have gone off overnight alone together in the last six months.

_____ I tell my mate verbally that I desire him or her.

_____ My mate would describe me as a tender lover.

_____ I'm willing to work on areas in our sexual relationship that need improvement.

If you checked seven or more of these statements, you most likely have a reasonably healthy sexual relationship. If your score was lower than seven, don't be discouraged. A candid self-appraisal and an effort to modify your attitude can result in a change in your score in a very short time! Note: On this SAT you can miss checking one of the statements and still be a ten.

God in the Bedroom

Most people did not grow up associating their sexuality with their relationship with God. But remember, the whole idea of being male and female and becoming one flesh was God's idea. Sexual intercourse originated in the Garden of Eden during the perfect, sinless state of humanity. Not only is God the creator of our sexuality and the sexual union between the husband and wife, but He is also vitally involved in our ongoing sexual lives when we allow Him to be.

Take some time to talk about how each of you view God's role in your bedroom. Discuss the following questions:

- Do you think God wants your sexual life to be full of spark?
- Does He care for you in times of sexual frustration, problems, and pain?
- Does He approve of your fun, wacky, and silly times of loving each other?

You may want to spend some time studying what the Scriptures teach about sex. We suggest that you read out loud together the Song of Solomon. You may want to use a contemporary translation. Each of you read the part for your sex. For example, in chapter 7, verses 10–12, the wife reads:

> I am my beloved's,
> And his desire is toward me.
> Come, my beloved,

Let us go forth to the field; ...
Let us get up early to the vineyards; ...
There I will give you my love.

When King Solomon speaks, the husband reads to his wife. Selections from chapter 7 are:

How beautiful are your feet in sandals,
O prince's daughter!
The curves of your thighs are like jewels,
The work of the hands of a skillful workman. (v. 1)
Your two breasts are like two fawns,
Twins of a gazelle. (v. 3)
How fair and how pleasant you are,
O love, with your delights! (v. 6)

What a beautiful way to express your love for each other—a true gift from God! After you have read together from the Song of Solomon, spend a few minutes in prayer and thank God for the gift of sex.[16] 🔖

Five Tips for Rekindling Your Love

1. Read the following paragraphs out loud together:

Be affectionate. Romance is not something to be saved just for the bedroom. Being thoughtful and kind at other times will spill over into your lovemaking. We all like to be nurtured and cherished. Phone calls, notes that say, "I love you," cooking your mate's favorite dish, giving a bouquet of flowers, and saying loving and endearing things to each other will add depth to your physical love.

"Sex begins outside the bedroom," says Evelyn Moschetta, D.S.W., a marriage counselor in New York City. "Physical and verbal affection, helping each other out, coming through for each other—that's what activates the warm, close, loving feelings you take into the bedroom."[17]

Be a listener. Really listen to each other and share your own feelings. One of the most important lovemaking skills is being able to listen with your heart and to talk to each other while you are making love. Your sex life may be active, but if it is all action and no talk, you're missing an added dimension of sharing and satisfaction. Try telling your mate what you like. Use a little body language. You aren't mind readers.

Be adventuresome. Try a little spontaneity. If you always make love in the evening, try mornings. Call in late for work and grab a couple of hours with each other after the kids go to school. Or plan a middle of the day rendezvous. Take a long lunch. Borrow the keys to a friend's condo for an afternoon of romance. Try some variety in when and where you make love. Remember variety can be the spice of life!

Be playful. Remember that getting there is half the fun. Making time for love will help you be good to each other, so take your time. You may need to unwind from your busy day, so make the transition slowly. Go for a walk and hold hands. Stop along the way for a kiss or two. Taking time to kiss and cuddle and to laugh and share intimate thoughts during your lovemaking will add to your ultimate pleasure.

Be thankful to God. Remember the sexual experience in marriage is a special gift from God. He designed our bodies with the capacity for pleasure, so relax and enjoy each other with God's blessing! Don't allow others who have distorted God's wonderful gift to color your experience or perspective.

2. Now, go back through each of these five tips and rate yourself in each area:

- I'm doing great in this area.
- I'm doing OK but can improve.
- I need to work on this one.

3. Compare your answers and choose one area to talk about in depth.

4. Make a list of practical steps you can take to improve in this area. 🦋

❧ Healthy Snacks ☙

Qualities of a Healthy Marriage

How healthy is your marriage? What are the most important qualities in your relationship? Go through the following list, and rate each quality on a scale from 1 to 10, 10 being the highest rating and 1 being the least satisfying rating. You may do this separately and then compare your ratings, or you may prefer to rate them together.

Here are marriage qualities to be rated:
1. A sense of belonging together
2. Good communication—really hearing each other, listening attentively, and expressing feelings and thoughts openly and honestly
3. Feeling good about each other and enjoying each other
4. Accepting and seeking to meet each other's needs
5. Feeling secure, safe, and trustful with each other
6. Depending on each other to honor agreements and commitments
7. Protecting each other against outside threats and judgments
8. Doing things together that are rewarding and enjoyable

Now you may want to start a dialogue on ways to improve the areas that you rated least satisfying. Agree on an area to start working on and go from there.   ↩

Taking a Marriage Inventory

Anytime is an appropriate time to take a marriage inventory. This exercise is designed to help you evaluate the state of your marriage as it is right now and look at ways you want it to grow.

We suggest you independently answer the following questions and then share your answers with each other. Then talk about what adjustments or changes you would like to make.

1. On a scale from 1 to 10, how would you rate the quality of your relationship?

2. What are the positive factors in your relationship?

3. What were your early expectations? Have they been met?

4. What has been the most difficult adjustment you have had to make together in your marriage?

5. What has helped the most in adjusting to each other in your marriage?

6. What changes do you need to make to keep growing together?

7. Has doing this exercise raised any new issues that you need to share with each other? ↩

Worship and Marriage

When couples are asked to list what makes their marriage strong, they frequently mention shared values and faith in God. Many couples report that their faith in God and religious practices are significant parts of their relationship. The following questions are designed to help you talk together as a couple about your spiritual life.

1. What religious experiences do you recall from your childhood and adolescence? Did you grow up in a religious home?

2. Are there experiences that have had special meaning to you (positive or negative)?

3. If you attended a church or synagogue during your childhood, what was it like?

4. How important was worship and religion in your home?

5. What religious practices took place at home? Who took responsibility for them? In what way were they meaningful? Or not meaningful?

6. Share with your mate what persons have had an influence on your spiritual development.

7. How important are spiritual issues in your marriage?

8. What questions of faith or meaning are you dealing with now?

9. Where are you in your spiritual pilgrimage?

10. Are there steps you would like to take to deepen your spiritual life?

Building Positive In-law Relationships

Judging from all the in-law jokes, in-law relationships may be among the most neglected and abused of all family relationships. How can you build a more positive relationship with your in-laws? The more mutual respect and enjoyment you experience with your mate's parents, the more security and stability you and your spouse will feel in your marriage.

If you'd like to maintain a growing friendship with your in-laws, here are some ideas you may want to try. Discuss them together and talk about what might work in your unique situation.

1. Write a letter to your partner's parents thanking them for a character trait or personal skill they instilled in your mate.

2. The next time you visit your in-laws' home, look for something you can do for them, maybe run an errand or help with a difficult circumstance or decision. What are some ways you could serve them?

3. If you live far apart and see them only infrequently, schedule a regular visit by phone. You may want to discuss how often you should call and how long your conversations should be.

Above all, remember to be grateful to your in-laws. They were the ones who provided the climate for cultivating all the attractive qualities in that unique person you chose to marry. Remember, in making that family tie stronger, you'll make your marriage stronger as well! ↵

How Are Your Coping Skills?

Following is a list of problem situations in marriage. To see how you are coping, go through the list and indicate to what extent each problem area has been present in your marriage.

Answer each problem situation with *often, sometimes,* or *never.* Then share your responses and talk about how well you have coped, or are coping, with these problems.

1. Money problems
2. Can't really talk to each other
3. Arguing, fighting
4. Sex problems
5. Disagreements about friends
6. Jealousy
7. Problems with children
8. Job problems
9. In-laws and relatives
10. Not enough time together
11. Religion
12. Care of the home
13. Health issues—yourself
14. Health issues—your partner
15. Health issues—your relatives

 NOTE: If there are areas in which you are not coping well, discuss possible avenues for help. A couple of hours with a Christian counselor can sometimes work wonders.

Community Service Project

To discover the joy of doing something for someone else without any thought of reward or recognition is a noble goal. The activity is also a marriage builder if you do it together as a couple. You learn a lot about each other when you work together on a project, whether it's building your own new home or helping build a home for Habitat for Humanity! Look around your community. Survey the needs and together choose a service project. You'll grow together as you help others.

Following is a list of possible projects. Use this list as a catalyst to come up with your own unique brand of service!

1. Choose an ecology project, start a neighborhood recycling program.

2. Give financial support and practical help to a family who is needy.

3. Lend a hand to an elderly neighbor (helping with yard work, shopping, providing transportation for doctors' appointments, reading, or just being available for conversation).

4. Help build a house for Habitat for Humanity.

5. Go on a short-term missions project.

6. Adopt a missionary family. Remember birthdays and anniversaries with small gifts.

7. Volunteer to teach Sunday school.

8. If you are both athletic, volunteer to coach a little league team.

9. Help with a soup kitchen or at a homeless shelter or at the Salvation Army.

10. Be an aunt and uncle to a child in a single-parent home.

Now add your own creative ideas!

Celebrations and Traditions

Have you created your own traditions and celebrations? Use this short exercise to look at your holidays and celebrations. Talk about the meaning of each holiday and how you celebrate it. Then decide together if any changes are in order to make them uniquely yours.

1. Talk about how each of your families observed holidays when you were children. Which were the most important? the least important?

2. What are some of the pleasant memories you still have? Are there some unpleasant memories associated with holidays?

3. What holiday traditions have special meaning to you personally?

4. What holiday activities create stress?

5. What activities do you look forward to?

6. Is there some tradition that one of you would like to discontinue?

7. Is there some tradition you would like to initiate?

Balancing Marriage, Family, and Work

Do you know anyone who hasn't struggled with work-related stress? It seems we always have too little time and energy left for our families. But work stress doesn't have to totally disrupt your marriage. Use this exercise as a starting point to help you and your spouse find ways to better balance your work life and your family life.[18]

1. Are there times when you derive more satisfaction from your work than you do from your home life?

If you answered "yes," what are the aspects of your work that you find more fulfilling than your responsibilities at home?

How can you find ways to generate a greater level of satisfaction from your family-related tasks?

2. Are you satisfied with the balance between the amount of time you devote to work and the number of hours you spend with your family?

If "no," is there anything you can do to free up more time for your spouse and children?

3. Are there specific times during the work week—or on a monthly or annual basis—that are especially stressful?

If "yes," what can each of you do to provide needed support to the other during times of high work stress?

4. Are you doing a good job of coping with your own work-related stress to keep it from negatively affecting your attitude at home?

If "no," how can you more effectively deal with your stress level?

5. Are you doing enough to include each other in your respective work worlds?

If "no," what can each of you do to involve the other more in your work world?

6. Do you have any unfulfilled career goals?

Preventing Moving Trauma

Is a move coming up in your near future? A move can reveal much about yourselves and your differences. One may grieve before the move and then adjust quickly afterwards. The other may breeze through the first process, but really feel a loss after the move is completed. You may have different packing styles and find one of you settles in quicker than the other.

In anticipating a move and to increase your understanding of each other, discuss the following questions:

1. What does this move mean to me? What are my dreams? fears? expectations?

2. What are the things I find most stressful in moving?

3. How long does it take me to adjust to major changes in my life? What is my grief pattern?

4. What things can we do as a couple to keep our bond strong during this time of confusion and upheaval?   ↬

The Ultimate Supper Club
with a Purpose

An Ultimate Supper Club is your opportunity to combine excellent cuisine, fun, Bible study, and enrichment for your marriage and the marriages of your friends! To encourage other couples to build their marital partnership, start your own Ultimate Supper Club. We suggest getting together with three other couples once a month for four months. The appendix gives you a step-by-step guide for organizing and leading your own Ultimate Supper Club. Use this exercise to brainstorm and get you started:

List other couples who might be interested in joining your Supper Club:

Couples we could ask are:

_____   _____

_____   _____

Possible date we could consider starting: _____

Choose a time when you could have prospective couples over to share the idea and talk._____

↬

Planning Future Getaways

If your Ultimate Marriage Builder Getaway has been enjoyable, you'll want to plan more of them in the future. To do just that, use the following planning guide.

1. Places we would like to go (make a list and then choose one):

2. Possible dates available (choose one and write it down in your calendar; you also may want to choose an alternate date):

3. Resources for this weekend (work out a budget; decide if this will be an economy getaway or the big splurge, five-star getaway):

4. Arrangements to make (child care, pet care, reservations, getting maps, arranging for someone to pick up mail and newspapers, etc.):

5. Packing list (things we want to take along; see The Getaway Box, pg. 10):

6. Write your own "Getaway Agreement" (see page 19).

7. Things we would like to talk about (review the Mini Marriage Builder Menu on page 102 and choose topics you want to discuss on your getaway). Then fill out the schedule on the following page for your weekend plan. (For your convenience, suggested exercises have been included.) ⟳

Ultimate Marriage Builder Getaway

Schedule for: _____

Date:_____   Location: _____

Depart:_____   Arrive: _____

Friday Night   <u>"Great Expectations" (119)</u>
                        _____
                        _____

Saturday Morning   <u>"Becoming Close Companions" (142)</u>
                        _____
                        _____

Saturday Afternoon   <u>"Leisure and Recreation in Marriage" (124)</u>
                        _____
                        _____

Saturday Night   <u>"What Now, My Love?" (172)</u>
                        _____
                        _____

Sunday   <u>"What's Your Marriage Potential? (110)</u>
                        _____
                        _____

Marriage Enrichment Opportunities

If this weekend has been fun, plan another one. We would like to recommend several resources that will help you do this.

Marriage Enrichment Organizations

United Marriage Encounter

A wonderful source for enriching your marriage relationship is United Marriage Encounter. United Marriage Encounter is a nondenominational Christian ministry offering weekend retreats to help good marriages become better and to help couples grow closer to each other and to God. They also offer continuing community groups for further growth and fellowship with other couples.

If you enjoyed this weekend getaway, then we know you would really benefit from a Marriage Encounter Weekend. You might consider this getaway as an appetizer for a full Marriage Encounter Weekend. We highly recommend it!

For more information about Marriage Encounter or to get a schedule of weekend encounters you may attend, contact:

United Marriage Encounter
P.O. Box 209
Muscatine, IA 52761

Association of Couples in Marriage Enrichment
(A.C.M.E.)

Also we wish to acknowledge A.C.M.E. and our dear friends David and Vera Mace for their contribution to our own marriage and their generosity in letting us share what they taught us with you. Many of the Mini Marriage Builders in this section are adapted from the A.C.M.E. newsletters we have benefited from over the years.

You can benefit too from this excellent marriage enrichment organization. A.C.M.E. was established in 1973 by the Maces and is a network of couples working for better marriages—beginning with their own. A.C.M.E. activities and resources focus on prevention and growth and include weekend retreats, local marriage growth groups, newlywed programs, and a practical newsletter.

We encourage you to become a member of A.C.M.E. You'll have the opportunity to experience new growth in your marriage. We highly recommend A.C.M.E. to you. Get involved! For more information contact:

A.C.M.E.
P.O. Box 10596
Winston-Salem, NC 27108

Marriage Alive

Our Marriage Alive workshop is a fun-filled, interactive, six-hour workshop to help you fine-tune your marriage. Topics covered include: High Priority Marriage, Finding Unity in Diversity, Communication, and Goal Setting. For information about hosting a Marriage Alive workshop, contact:

Marriage Alive
P.O. Box 90303
Knoxville, TN 37990
(615) 691–8505

Magazines

Magazines have great ideas to help you build your marriage. Consider the ones listed here.

Marriage Partnership

We also highly recommend *Marriage Partnership* magazine as an excellent resource for enriching your marriage. Each issue (published quarterly) contains several Marriage Builders that are fun, positive, and easy to discuss. We wish to thank *Marriage Partnership* for giving us permission to use several of their Marriage Builders in this section. To subscribe to *Marriage Partnership*, write to:

Marriage Partnership
P.O. Box 11618
Des Moines, IA 50340

Christian Parenting Today

Another very helpful resource is *Christian Parenting Today*. In each issue we challenge you to build your marriage in our regular column

"You and Your Spouse." Several of the Mini Marriage Builders are adapted from our columns in *Christian Parenting Today.*

Because our parenting role is so intertwined with our marriage partnership role, we feel that if we enrich our family we will also enrich our marriage. Many of the issues we face today in marriage are tied to parenting. To receive valuable information and encouragement for your family, subscribe to *Christian Parenting Today* by writing to:

Christian Parenting Today
P.O. Box 545
Mt. Morris, IL 61054–0545

NOTE: If you mention our name and the code Z-60, *Christian Parenting Today* will send you a free issue of the magazine. If you choose to subscribe you will receive the special Ultimate Marriage Builder discount rate of $12.95 per year. But you must give the code Z-60!

PART FOUR

AFTER
THE
GETAWAY

One to two weeks after your getaway weekend

Chapter Nine

Looking Back and Looking Forward

"Is it Monday already? The weekend flew by, and now reality has set back in. Back to work, school, kids, and all the other things that are a part of our busy lives; but we're happy to say, after our weekend away, we're facing them with a much better attitude!"

Married eleven years, two children

Did your getaway weekend just zip by? Did things at home accelerate while you were gone? It's easy to feel a little overwhelmed. Good plans and intentions can be lost in the shuffle of real life. That's why we encouraged you to plan a Time for Two within the first two weeks after your weekend. We hope that's where you are (or getting ready to be) right now!

First, spend a little time enjoying the memories of your personal Ultimate Marriage Builder just-for-two encounter weekend. Here's an opportunity to affirm and complement the positive changes you have already observed.

Before your getaway, we suggested playing "I'm looking forward to . . ." Hopefully, that little exercise helped you verbalize your expectations and got you off to a good start. Carl and Louise, married twenty years and raising three teenagers, said it was helpful to them—both before and after their getaway. They told us, "This exercise is excellent! We plan to play 'I'm looking forward to' before every getaway and every family vacation. In fact, with three teenagers in our house, we should probably do it every Friday night in preparation for the weekend."

TIME FOR REMEMBERING

Playing "I remember" can also be helpful. It can give you a positive attitude about your future as you remember times of closeness and commitments you made.

Separately, make a list of things you remember from your getaway. Then share your lists with each other. To help you remember, look back through your Weekend Notebook. Then talk about it.

If you did not do the exercise Looking Back and Looking Forward on pages 93–96, take the time right now to do it. Even if you went through this exercise at the end of your weekend, pull it out again and review it.

Remember to give each other time to ease back into the sharing and talking mode. One wife said her husband loved to talk but that he was like an old pump that had to be primed! So if one of you is a more aggressive talker, give the other time to formulate his or her thoughts without being interrupted.

Did your weekend include problem solving? Were there issues you resolved? Are there some issues you still need to resolve? Identifying a problem is half the battle, especially if you can attack it and not each other. However, sometimes we need a third party to help us get turned around. If you can't seem to resolve a problem on your own, talking with a caring professional may be a very positive step. We encourage you to take the next step and get the help you need if this is your situation.

LOOKING FORWARD

After you complete or review the Looking Back and Looking Forward exercise, focus on the next twelve months and consider ten areas of your life. The following exercise, The Next 12 Months, will help you do just that.

The Next 12 Months[19]

Where will your marriage be in 12 months?

Choose several of the following ten categories you need to work on and then set goals in those areas for the coming year. Ask yourself in each area, "Where do we want our marriage to be in twelve months?"

1. Your Marriage Relationship

Are you both content with the styles and the level of your communication? Are you satisfied with the way you resolve issues? How are you doing at processing anger? Do you feel you spend enough time alone together? Are you satisfied with your love life?

List some specific goals you would like to achieve:

_____

_____

_____

_____

2. Your Children

Do you want to deepen your relationship with your children? Do you spend one-on-one time with each child on a regular basis? Have you both set mutual goals for your family? Are you satisfied with your children's spiritual training and growth, their academic progress, their friendships, and the development of their talents and abilities? Can you identify specific areas that need additional attention?

List some specific goals you would like to achieve:

_____

_____

_____

_____

3. Your Personal Discipleship

Are you satisfied with your spiritual growth, both individually and as a couple? Do you need to make any changes in your shared or private devotional life? Do you often pray together?

List some specific goals you would like to achieve:

_____

_____

_____

_____

4. Your Careers

Discuss your level of income and job satisfaction. What stresses do you face in your job and what can you do to offset them? What are your opportunities for career growth? Are there practical steps you can take to achieve them? Are there life-style issues you need to discuss?

List some specific goals you would like to achieve:

_____

_____

_____

_____

5. Managing Family Finances

Do you have a workable budget? Are you in debt? Do you have a realistic plan for becoming debt free? Do you both feel comfortable with your rate of savings? Are you saving for college for your children, for a family vacation? Are you reserving funds for emergencies, for retirement? Do you need to reevaluate your insurance coverage? Are you comfortable with your level of charitable giving, as well as the amount of money you devote to hobbies and other leisure activities?

List some specific goals you would like to achieve:

_____

_____

_____

_____

6. Your Leisure Activities

Is enough leisure time scheduled into your family's calendar? Are you satisfied with the amount of time you devote to each other in dates, special celebrations, and getaway weekends? Do you set aside enough time for recreation that you both enjoy?

List some specific goals you would like to achieve:

_____

_____

_____

_____

7. Your Extended Family

Are you both satisfied with the amount of time you spend with your parents, siblings, and other relatives? Do you have any family members who might need more of your attention this year? Do you have financial concerns related to gift giving or to caring for elderly parents?

List some specific goals you would like to achieve:

_____

_____

_____

_____

8. Your Church Involvement

How many hours a week do you spend at church—too few or too many? Are you satisfied with your financial giving to the church? Are you personally involved in supporting a missionary family or a local cause? If not, would you like to be? Are you able to make use of your personal talents in a church-related ministry?

List some specific goals you would like to achieve:

_____

_____

_____

_____

9. Personal Growth as Individuals

Are there specific ways you want to grow personally this year? What are your dreams? Do you get regular exercise? Do you devote enough time to developing your individual friendships? Do you want to take a class related to your career or a favorite hobby? Do you want to do more reading?

List some specific goals you would like to achieve:

_____

_____

_____

_____

10. Your Community Involvement

Are there outreach needs in your community that you would like to pursue? How do you feel about your role in your neighborhood? Are you satisfied with your children's schools? Are you involved in your children's schools as a volunteer? Are you involved in community clubs and organizations, or would you like to be?

List some specific goals you would like to achieve:

_____

_____

_____

SIX MONTHS FROM NOW

After writing out your goals in the areas you have chosen, pick an evening six months from now to review together how you are doing on reaching your goals. Make any mid-course adjustments you need to make.

You may even want to plan a getaway together a year from now (or even in six months) to celebrate your successes and the goals you have achieved. Then dream new dreams and set new goals for your ultimate marriage!

WHAT NOW?

Your goals for the next twelve months are formulated, and your memories from your fun getaway are cataloged. Perhaps you've worked through some issues in your relationship, and you are pleased with the progress you have made. You have stirred up your own marriage with positive results. What do you do now? To continue growing, we challenge you to help other marriages grow too!

In the last Mini Marriage Builder, Marriage Enrichment Opportunities, we challenged you to get involved with an organization that is committed to helping marriages grow. We recommended several marriage enrichment opportunities like a Marriage Encounter or A.C.M.E. Marriage Enrichment Weekend or our own Marriage Alive Workshop. We also recommended several magazines that can be a periodical reminder to celebrate your marriage. We have one last suggestion: Start an Ultimate Supper Club!

THE ULTIMATE SUPPER CLUB

Today most of us have more demands than time. As a result, time with other couples may be neglected. Yet we know how important it is in our own marriage to have supportive and encouraging couple friendships. We are there for each other in the hard times, and at other times we enjoy one another's successes. If presently you don't have supportive couple relationships, you can develop them. You can start an Ultimate Supper Club! We can even tell you how.

An Ultimate Supper Club can be whatever you want it to be, but here is our suggestion. Find several other couples (three other couples works well) and form a supper club. You could get together once a month for four months. That works out to be one dinner for each couple to plan and host.

While the cuisine may be appealing, the unique thing about the Ultimate Supper Club is that it is also good for your health—your marital health! While enjoying the food, fun, and fellowship, you'll have the opportunity to focus on your marriage, with a unique blend of fun and purpose.

To make your Ultimate Supper Club easy to lead, we suggest using our book *The Marriage Track*. The study guide in the next chapter gives you all you need to use *The Marriage Track* effectively with your friends. Dinnertime conversation starters keep you on your topic, and after-dinner Bible studies give you God's perspective on marriage. Easy-to-follow sessions guidelines help you stay on track. Bible studies and questions and exercises give you insight into your relationship with each other and God. Check it out; you'll find this is a way to celebrate your marriage and help other couples as well!

TAKE THE RISK

Are you willing to take the risk to keep your love alive? Are you willing to trust God during the hard times? Are you willing to intentionally work at keeping fun, intimacy, and romance alive in your marriage? Are you willing to share what you have found with others?

If you answer yes to all of these questions, then we're willing to say you have an ultimate marriage!

PART FIVE

APPENDICES

The Ultimate Supper Club

Welcome to the Ultimate Supper Club. This is your opportunity to combine good food and good times with making good progress in enriching your own marriage and encouraging other couples to do the same!

Today most of us have more demands on us than time to meet them. When we are under stress and pressure, the two things that tend to go are fun with friends and fun times with each other. According to a recent survey of couples who have attended our Marriage Alive Workshops, we are not alone. The top two needs that surfaced in this survey are 1) more time for fun, and 2) time to grow toward a strong partnership in their marriage. The Ultimate Supper Club offers both!

The Ultimate Supper Club lets you have fun while helping to meet several key needs such as:

- providing for the development of supportive relationships with other like-minded couples.

- providing practical Bible studies for building a strong marriage partnership.
- learning by doing through exercises, discussions with other couples, and dates with your mate.

STARTING AN ULTIMATE
SUPPER CLUB

How do you start an Ultimate Supper Club? You just do it! It's simple, and we will gladly walk you through the process of four fun-filled dinners with your friends. What a great way to encourage your friends while building your own marriage.

All you need are a few couples (three other couples is ideal) and four evenings (we suggest once a month). We will even give you suggested menus (see page 231). Again it's your choice what you eat and what you do to build your marriages, but we will offer our favorite suggestions.

The following guide is designed to help make your role as the Ultimate Supper Club organizer easy and enjoyable. It's based on our family's favorite menus and two of our favorite books, *The Marriage Track* and *52 Dates for You and Your Mate* (both available from Thomas Nelson Publishers). You can also supplement your supper club with the Mini Marriage Builders in chapter 8 of this book.

Each couple will need their own copy of *The Marriage Track*, *52 Dates for You and Your Mate*, and a photocopy of the couple's study in this book. Only you will need this simple-to-follow leader's guide. Relax. We will give you all the tools and tips you need to make this a fun supper club with a purpose!

Supper Club Activities

Each Ultimate Supper Club Dinner Plan will include dinner time conversation starters and enhancers based on the topic of the evening. We hope they will bring out humor, fun, and laughter. (It helps if you make sure you have at least one or more humorous persons in your group!)

The second part of the evening includes a practical after-dinner Bible study (thirty to forty minutes) which covers topics that are critical to building a strong marriage partnership. Topics include commitment, respect and unity, communication, and having a common vision that is bigger than the two of you! Scripture verses are given for each study. You can also close out each evening with a "side-track" time when you can choose any topic the group wants to talk about.

To continue the fun, part of the assignment between dinners is to plan and have a date with your mate. This is where the book *52 Dates for You and Your Mate* enters in. You can choose from seven different kinds of dates depending on your budget (there are cheap and easy dates), energy (there are "I'm just too tired" dates), or how amorous you feel (of course, there are romantic dates!).

Us Lead This?

If you're thinking, "We're not sure we can lead this," don't panic. Sure you can and we're giving you all the helps that you need. For each evening there are session guidelines with questions and possible answers. You can't beat that! And remember, you are a team—you have each other to rely on!

There is an Ultimate Supper Club Agreement (on page 232) for each couple to sign. In signing, they agree to do their part (to prepare and to participate) and to keep the evening's conversation confidential. This helps the group to grow together and trust one another. It makes your job as facilitator and organizer much easier. We suggest that you present the agreement to the group at this introductory evening.

Don't forget to give the first assignment before you leave.

For a fun beginning to your upcoming first session, ask each couple to bring one of their wedding pictures (not the whole album please!), or a picture from before they were married. Ask them to read *The Marriage Track*, chapters 1 and 2, and do the exercises. Ask them to also do the Bible study in Session One, and suggest they have a date.

Enjoy the rest of the evening with your friends and talk about how much fun your Ultimate Supper Club is going to be!

The first step is to choose the other couples who would like to join your Ultimate Supper Club. Make a list of couples you could ask to be in your supper club:

_____   _____

_____   _____

You'll want to list more couples than you need since everyone may not be able to participate. The next step is to talk it up and form your group. Choose an evening to have everyone over for dessert and to talk about launching your supper club. This will be a good time to choose in whose home your club will meet and when. You can use the Ultimate Supper Club schedule on page 229 to help you plan. If you want to use our dinner selections, you can pass them out. If you have a bunch of creative gourmets, skip our suggestions and do your own thing.

The Introductory Evening

At the introductory get-together pass out copies of *The Marriage Track* and the Bible studies (that you have photocopied). Each partner should have his or her own copy of the Bible study.

After the Fourth—What Then?

If your Supper Club is so much fun—you just don't want to stop after four dinners—by all means keep going! You may want to set up four more. You can continue through *The Marriage Track*. (At this point, you will have finished Part 1 of the book.) You can plan your own evening with the Ultimate Mini Marriage Builders or you can use our book *60 One-Minute Marriage Builders*.

At this point, you may want to pass around the responsibility of leading the group from couple to couple.

We know you are eager to get started, so turn to page 231 for the study! The Leader's Guide follows on page 247. We know you can do it!

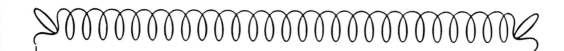

Ultimate Supper Club Schedule

Session	Date	Time	Location	Hostess	(Leader)
One					
Two					
Three					
Four					

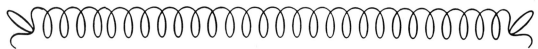

Session One

Suggested Dinner Menus

Italian Extravaganza
Homemade Pizza and Bruchetta
Linguine with White Clam Sauce
Caesar Salad
Biscotti (Italian cookies, Yum!)

Easy Feast
Raw Vegetables & Dip
Honey-baked Ham
Potato Salad (from your favorite deli)
Corn on the Cob
Green Beans
Rolls
Ice Cream

Try Vegetarian
Roquefort Quiche
Fruit Salad
Whole Wheat Bread
Vegetable Medley
Chocolates & Coffee

Never Enough Italian
Minestrone Soup
Manicotti
Garlic bread
Gelato

The Ultimate Supper Club Agreement

As a member of this supper club we agree to:

- Read the chapter(s) for each session and complete the exercises and Bible study.

- Try to have at least one date between each supper club evening and the next.

- Keep all conversations positive during each evening. (The supper club is not a time to publicly resolve conflict.)

- Keep confidential any personal things that might be shared among the group.

- Host one of the dinners.

Signed_____ Date_____

Signed_____ Date_____

This agreement is to be signed and kept by each couple.

Couple's Study

Session One

Making Your Marriage a High Priority

Date and Location of Supper Club: _____

_____

_____

Assignment (before supper club):
1. Have a fun date!
2. Read chapters 1 and 2 of *The Marriage Track* and do exercises.
3. Complete the Bible study in Session One.
4. Bring wedding picture.

PART I. Getting your marriage on track

Read Ecclesiastes 4:9–12. This Scripture passage talks about a cord of three strands. In one former group studying the passage was a boat captain. He shared how the lines that tie the boat to the dock have to have three strands to keep from unraveling. "If one strand breaks," he said, "it all comes apart." How do these verses apply to marriage?

1. What are the three strands of the marriage cord? What happens when one breaks?

_____

_____

_____

2. According to verse 12, what are the benefits of having three strands?

_____

_____

_____

3. List some of the benefits of being "two."

_____

_____

_____

4. What are practical ways (besides keeping warm) that you can reap these benefits in your marriage?

_____

_____

_____

Can you share a recent experience?

_____

_____

_____

5. In the great context of Solomon's experience and wisdom, how does this passage relate to your marriage as a *friendship*? What are other

principles for building your friendship and intimacy in your marriage relationship?

_____

_____

_____

PART II. Making your marriage a high priority

Read Genesis 2:24. This verse mentions three principles—leaving, cleaving, and becoming one flesh. Most couples have at least one family of origin with intergenerational issues that interfere with their marriage. Often, the problem can be traced to ignoring the principles in this verse.

1. How did you leave? What did you leave or give a lower priority?

_____

_____

_____

2. What do you do that helps pull you together as a couple?

_____

_____

_____

3. How are you growing together?

_____

_____

_____

Session Two

Find Unity in Diversity

Date and Location of Supper Club: _____

_____

_____

Assignment (before supper club):
1. Have a fun date!
2. Read chapter 3 of *The Marriage Track*, and do the exercises.
3. Do the Bible study in Session Two.

PART I. Judging

Unity is one requirement for teamwork. One hindrance to unity, however, is judging your spouse.

Read Matthew 7:3–5

1. What causes us at times to focus on the speck in our spouse's eye? What are ways to avoid this?

_____

_____

_____

2. Is it wrong to desire the speck to be removed? Why?

_____

_____

_____

3. What actions are necessary to remove the log from our own eyes?

_____

_____

_____

PART II. Finding unity in diversity

1. In what areas are you different?

_____

_____

_____

2. In what areas are you alike?

_____

_____

_____

3. What are some practical ways in which you balance and compensate?

_____

_____

_____

PART III. Understanding gender differences

Read Genesis 5:1–2.

1. God made us male and female. How do gender differences affect our marriage relationship? While there are some stereotypes, what are some valid differences in the sexes?

_____

_____

_____

2. In our marriage, which of our differences seem to be personality differences and which seem to be gender related?

_____

_____

_____

Session Three

Improving Our Communication

Date and Location of Supper Club: _____

_____

_____

Assignment (before supper club):
1. Have a fun date!
2. Read chapters 4 and 5 in *The Marriage Track* and do the exercises.
3. Complete the Bible study in Session Three.

PART I. Quick to hear and slow to speak

The study deals with communicating our feelings—both the positive and the negative. One key is that we must do it very carefully!

Read James 1:19. This verse gives some helpful advice on communicating. What are practical ways that we do each?

1. How can we be quick to listen?

_____

_____

_____

2. How can we be slower to speak?

_____
_____
_____

3. How can we be slow to become angry?

_____
_____
_____

PART II. Healthy communication in marriage

Ephesians 4:29–32 has much to say about healthy communication that we can apply to our marriages.

Read Ephesians 4:29–32.

1. This passage also deals with anger and how we can get rid of it. Discuss these three steps and the corresponding Scripture.

Step 1: Acknowledge your anger as soon as you are aware of it (v. 31).

Step 2: Renounce your right to vent your anger at your mate (v. 29).

Step 3: Ask for your mate's help in dealing with your anger and the situation that is causing it (v. 32).

2. From this passage in Ephesians 4, how can we meet our mate's need for affirmation? How can we build each other up?

_____

_____

_____

3. How can we grieve the Holy Spirit in our conversations?

_____

_____

_____

PART III. Thoughts and attitudes

Philippians 4:4–9 can help us control our attitudes and thoughts.

Read Philippians 4:4–9.

1. What attitudes do we need to foster that will help us to communicate the positive? (What opposite attitudes do we need to avoid?)

_____

_____

_____

2. What is one of your mate's most endearing qualities?

_____

Session Four

Setting Goals for Your Marriage

Date and Location of Supper Club: _____

_____

_____

_____

Assignment (before supper club):
1. Have a fun date!
2. Read chapter 6, in *The Marriage Track*, and do the exercises.
3. Complete Bible study in Session Four.

PART I. Dreaming about the future

It is fun to plan, to fantasize, to dream about the future. It is also biblical. Setting goals involved choices. Joshua set a goal for himself and his household to serve the Lord and his goal involved choices.

Read Joshua 24:14–18.

Joshua's goal was to serve the Lord.

1. From these verses, what foundational principles can we find for setting goals that are biblical?

_____

_____

_____

2. What are the gods of the 1990s?

_____

_____

_____

3. What has God provided for us in the past?

_____

_____

_____

4. Read Jeremiah 29:11. Why should we trust that God's way is best?

_____

_____

_____

PART II. Setting goals

Read 2 Timothy 4:7–8.

1. Paul speaks of finishing the race. Relate this to your marriage. What do you want yours to look like at the finish line? Do you know an older couple (actually it could also be a couple your age or younger) who

have the kind of relationship that you would like to have someday? What qualities would you like to have?

_____

_____

_____

2. Consider this description of Christian marriage as described by Tertullian in the second century:

> How beautiful is the marriage of two Christians, two who are one in hope, one in desire, one in the way of life they follow, one in the religion they practice.... Nothing divides them, either in flesh or in spirit. They pray together; instructing one another, encouraging one another, strengthening one another.... They have no secrets from one another; they never shun each other's company; they never bring sorrow to each other's hearts. They visit the sick and assist the needy. Psalms and hymns they sing to one another, striving to see which of them will chant more beautifully the praises of their Lord. Hearing and seeing this, Christ rejoices. To such as these He gives His peace. Where there are two together there also He is present.[20]

What qualities from this quotation describe your marriage?

_____

_____

_____

What qualities from this quotation would you like to describe your relationship in the future?

_____

_____

_____

3. In 2 Timothy 4:7, Paul reflects on his life and is able to speak confidently about his accomplishments. Relate this to your marriage. What are things that you must fight, for or against, in order to maintain a healthy Christian marriage?

_____

_____

_____

4. To fight the fight and finish the race requires keeping the faith. Referring to Ecclesiastes 4:9–12, what are practical ways that we keep the faith in our marriage?

_____

_____

_____

PART III. Making it personal

Complete this exercise for your own personal growth. These responses will not be shared in the group unless you want to share them.

To help you think about the goals you might want to have in your marriage, complete the following questions.

Appendix
Two

1. What do I want for me?

_____

_____

_____

2. What do I want for you?

_____

_____

_____

3. What do I want for us?

_____

_____

_____

Based on your answers and discussions choose goals you want to set for your marriage.

Long-Term Goals:

_____

_____

_____

Short-Term Goals:

_____

_____

_____

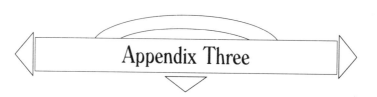

Leader's Guide

Session One

Making Your Marriage a High Priority

Purpose: The most important objective of this first evening is simply to break the ice and set the stage for fun. You can do this by asking the couples to share the lighter side of their wedding experience. The second purpose is to help the couples understand and apply the three basic principles of a growing marriage (leaving, cleaving, and becoming one flesh).

Preparation:
1. Read *The Marriage Track*, chapters 1 and 2, and do the exercises.
2. Have a date.
3. Do the Bible study in Session One.
4. Find a wedding picture to take to the group.

DINNER DISCUSSION

Ask each couple to describe how and when they first met and their fondest or funniest memory of their wedding day. If they brought a picture of their wedding, enjoy passing these around. To give each couple time, you may need to keep the discussion moving around the table. The purpose is to help people get to know each other better and, hopefully, help them to feel comfortable sharing during this evening and on future evenings.

STUDY

Chapter 1 is Getting Your Marriage on Track. To start the study you might want to emphasize the importance of staying "on track." You could share a time when you and your spouse got lost and relate the frustrations you experienced when you were not on track. Try to make it humorous so that people will feel free to share.

Next, lead discussion for Bible study. The study and discussion questions, with possible answers, follow.

PART I. Getting your marriage on track

Have someone read Ecclesiastes 4:9–12. This scripture passage talks about a cord of three strands. A boat captain was in one group studying the passage. He shared how the lines that tie the boat to the dock have to have three strands to keep from unraveling. "If one strand breaks," he said, "it all comes apart." How do these verses apply to marriage?

1. What are the three strands of the marriage cord? What happens when one breaks?

The husband, the wife, and the Lord

Things easily begin to unravel and come apart!

2. According to verse 12, what are the benefits of having three strands?

A cord of three strands is not quickly broken. In engineering, this is called fatigue strength.

It won't unravel!

3. List some of the benefits of being "two."

Good return for their work (v. 9) (i.e., good return on their investment)

One can help the other in time of need (v. 10)

Two can defend and support each other (v. 12)

4. What are practical ways (besides keeping warm) that you can reap these benefits in your marriage?

Work together by having common goals

Take advantage of each partner's strengths _____

Praise each other in public, never criticize _____

Can you share a recent experience?

_____

_____

_____

5. In the context of Solomon's experience and wisdom, how does this passage relate to your marriage as a *friendship*? What are other principles for building friendship and intimacy in your marriage relationship?

Friends have fun together. _____

Friends share their inner feelings with each other. _____

Intimate friends work through their problems. _____

PART II. Making your marriage a high priority

Have someone read Genesis 2:24. This verse mentions three principles—leaving, cleaving, and becoming one flesh. Most couples have at least one family of origin with intergenerational issues that interfere with their marriage. Often, the problem can be traced to ignoring the principles in this verse.

1. How did you leave? What did you leave or give a lower priority?

Parents, other relationships

Established financial security, etc.

2. What do you do that helps pull you together as a couple?

Prayer time, dates

Standing together against opposition

3. How are you growing together?

Understanding personal needs

Developing intimacy

PART III. Winding down

1. Have a side-track time. If there is time and interest, talk about whatever the group wants to talk about.

2. Review the following assignment for the next supper club and remind the couples of the date, time, and place you will meet.

* Have a fun date!

* Read chapter 3 and do the exercises. Complete the Bible study in Session Two.

3. Close in prayer.

Session Two

Finding Unity in Diversity

Purpose: Couples will learn how we can balance or compensate for differing or similar personalities and the importance of acceptance and forgiveness.

Preparation:
1. Read *The Marriage Track*, chapter 3, and do the exercises.
2. Have a fun date.
3. Do the Bible study in Session Two.
4. Prepare place cards (cut paper 3" x 8" and fold in half).

Scripture: Matthew 7:3–5; Genesis 5:1–2

DINNER DISCUSSION

Chapter 3 discusses different types of personalities we and our spouses might have and how we must balance or compensate for each other depending on whether we are alike or different. For fun during the dinner time ask everyone what type of animal best represents their personality. Have everyone tell what qualities made them choose this animal. It might be fun to have 3" x 8" inch pieces of paper available at the place settings and let everyone write the animal name on the paper and lay it face down. Go around the table letting each person introduce the animal they chose and fold the paper lengthwise making a name plate for their place setting.

STUDY

To begin the discussion, share a way in which you and your spouse are similar and a way in which you are different. Tell how you balance and compensate. How do you react to each other? Do you have any little irritating habits? (For example, Dave pauses to clip his fingernails while Claudia worries about being late to catch their plane!)

Lead the discussion for Bible study. The study and discussion questions, with possible answers, follow.

PART I. Judging

Unity is one requirement for teamwork. One hindrance to unity, however, is judging your spouse.

Have someone read Matthew 7:3–5.

1. What causes us at times to focus on the speck in our spouse's eye? What are ways to avoid this?

Frustration can cause us to be critical.

Our own insecurity magnifies our mate's speck.

Low self-esteem leads us to look for our spouse's faults.

2. Is it wrong to desire the speck to be removed? Why?

It is not wrong to want to remove the speck if our motive is love and concern and not judgmental.

Verse 5 says "then you will see clearly to remove the speck from your brother's eye."

3. What actions are necessary to remove the log from our own eyes?

First, realize it exists.

Second, understand its source (i.e., frustration, insecurity, low self-esteem).

In the future, try to avoid situations that bring about these feelings.

Pray and ask God to help you "see clearly." Then and only then can you help your mate.

PART II. Finding unity in diversity

1. In what areas are you different?

_____

_____

_____

2. In what areas are you alike?

_____

_____

_____

3. What are some practical ways in which you balance and compensate?

If you are struggling with opposite traits, try to think of them as complementary rather than competitive.

Realize that if your mate is strong in an area, that's a strength of your marriage team!

_____

PART III. Understanding gender differences

Have someone read Genesis 5:1–2.

1. God made us male and female. How do gender differences affect our marriage relationship? While there are some stereotypes, what are some valid differences in the sexes?

_____

_____

_____

2. In our marriage, which of our differences seem to be personality differences and which seem to be gender related?

_____

_____

_____

PART IV. Winding down

1. Have a side-track time. If there is time and interest, talk about whatever the group wants to talk about.

2. Review the following assignment for the next supper club and remind the couples of the date, time, and place you will meet.
  * Have a fun date!
  * Read chapters 4 and 5 in _The Marriage Track_ and do the exercises.
  * Complete the Bible study in Session Three.

3. Close in prayer.

Session Three

Improving Our Communication

Purpose: Help couples increase teamwork by improving communication and learning ways to communicate the positive.

Preparation:

1. Read *The Marriage Track*, chapters 4 and 5, and do the exercises.

2. Have a fun date.

3. Do the Bible study in Session Three.

Scripture: James 1:19; Ephesians 4:29–32; Philippians 4:4–9

DINNER DISCUSSION

Communication is such a broad subject that you can feel free to come up with your own discussion starter. Perhaps you've just heard a great joke or had a funny experience.

You might want to share nicknames you had as a child. Often they reflect your mode of communication, like the person who was known as the "motor mouth" or the "turtle."

Since nonverbal communication is so important, it might be fun to let everyone discuss their favorite method of positive nonverbal communication, such as kissing, hugging, or winking from across the room. Or ask, "How does your mate say I love you without saying a word?" It's important that you keep this part of the conversation on a positive track! You can deal with processing anger later in the Bible study.

STUDY

Begin the study by sharing a funny story about trying to communicate with someone.

Lead the discussion for Bible study. The study and discussion questions, with possible answers, follow.

PART I. Quick to hear and slow to speak

This study deals with communicating our feelings—both the positive and the negative. One key is that we must do it very carefully!

Have someone read James 1:19. This verse gives some helpful advice on communicating. What are practical ways that we do each?

1. How can we be quick to listen?

Set aside time, eliminate distractions.

Put your mate's concerns above your own.

Maintain eye contact.

2. How can we be slower to speak?

Realize that listening rather than speaking may be what is needed.

Pray before we speak in sensitive situations.

Listen for the real message.

3. How can we be slow to become angry?

Understand: "For man's anger does not bring about the righteous life that God desires" (v. 20, NIV).

If we are quick to listen and slow to speak, then perhaps we will be slow to get angry.

PART II. Healthy communication in marriage

Ephesians 4:29–32 has much to say about healthy communication that we can apply to our marriages.

Have someone read Ephesians 4:29–32.

1. This passage also deals with anger and how we can get rid of it. Discuss these three steps and the corresponding Scripture.

Step 1: Acknowledge your anger as soon as you are aware of it (v. 31).

Step 2: Renounce your right to vent your anger at your mate (v. 29).

Step 3: Ask for your mate's help in dealing with your anger and the situation that is causing it (v. 32).

See Mini Marriage Builder "Learning to Process Anger," on page 147. You may want to make an agreement to help each other process and get rid of anger whenever it appears!

2. From this passage in Ephesians 4, how can we meet our mate's need for affirmation? How can we build each other up?

Be kind.

Be compassionate.

Be forgiving.

3. How can we grieve the Holy Spirit in our conversations?

Being unkind

Being bitter

Not processing anger

PART III. Thoughts and attitudes

Philippians 4:4–9 can help us control our attitudes and thoughts.

Have someone read Philippians 4:4–9.

1. What attitudes do we need to foster that will help us to communicate the positive? (What opposite attitudes do we need to avoid?)

(v. 4) Attitude of rejoicing; avoid complaining

(v. 5) Gentleness; avoid harshness

Prayer and trust; avoid worry and anxiety

2. Let everyone share one of their mate's most endearing qualities with the group. Everyone likes affirmation, and everyone can surely think of one thing they like about their mate! It's a great way to end this Bible study!

PART IV. Winding down

1. Have a side-track time. If there is time and interest, talk about whatever the group wants to talk about.
2. Review the assignment for the next supper club dinner.
* Have a fun date!
* Read chapter 6 in *The Marriage Track* and do the exercises.
* Complete the Bible study in Session Four.
3. Close in prayer.

Session Four

Setting Goals for Your Marriage

Purpose: Couples will reexamine their expectations for their marriage, evaluate where their marriage is, and set realistic marriage goals.

Preparation:

1. Have a fun date!
2. Read *The Marriage Track*, chapter 6, and do the exercises.
3. Do the Bible study in Session Four.

Scripture: Joshua 24:14–18; Jeremiah 29:11; 2 Timothy 4:7

DINNER DISCUSSION

Let each couple share where they would go for an Ultimate Getaway Weekend if money and time were not a consideration.

Ask each person, "What gift would you give to your mate?"

Again, if finances were not an issue, where would you retire and what would you like to do? at sixty-five? at seventy-five? at eighty-five? at ninety?

Goals are important, and dreams are too. Many times, our goals will start out as dreams and this is an evening for both! Have fun dreaming at dinner. The realistic goal setting will come later!

STUDY

We set goals in business, why not in our marriages? The study this evening will deal with setting goals for our marriages that are in line with biblical principles and in light of eternity. Our biggest challenge is to set together goals that are bigger than the two of us.

Part of setting goals for the future is looking at where we have come in the past. (You may want to discuss the exercises on expectations from chapter 6. Just be sensitive that you don't allow the couples to become too personal or be embarrassed.) You could start the discussion by sharing a goal you set in the past and have actually achieved.

Lead the discussion for Bible study. The study and discussion questions, with possible answers, follow.

PART I. Dreaming about the future

It is fun to plan, to fantasize, to dream about the future. It is also biblical. Setting goals involves choices. Joshua set a goal for himself and his household to serve the Lord and his goal involved choices.

Have someone read Joshua 24:14–18.

Joshua's goal was to serve the Lord.

1. From these verses, what foundational principles can we find for setting goals that are biblical?

Fear the Lord (consider, reverence the Lord).

Serve the Lord faithfully.

Freely choose God's way.

2. What are the gods of the 1990s?

possessions

position

pleasure

3. What has God provided for us in the past?

provisions

protection

peace

4. Have someone read Jeremiah 29:11. Why should we trust that God's way is best?

He knows the future.

He plans for us to prosper.

He gives us hope and a future.

265

PART II. Setting goals

Have someone read 2 Timothy 4:7–8.

1. Paul speaks of finishing the race. Relate this to your marriage. What do you want yours to look like at the finish line? Do you know an older couple (actually it could also be a couple your age or younger) who have the kind of relationship that you would like to have someday? What qualities would you like to have?

friendship _____

oneness _____

faithfulness _____

2. Consider this description of Christian marriage as described by Tertullian in the second century:

How beautiful is the marriage of two Christians, two who are one in hope, one in desire, one in the way of life they follow, one in the religion they practice. . . . Nothing divides them, either in flesh or in spirit. They pray together; instructing one another, encouraging one another, strengthening one another. . . . They have no secrets from one another; they never shun each other's company; they never bring sorrow to each other's hearts. They visit the sick and assist the needy. Psalms and hymns they sing to one another, striving to see which of them will chant more beautifully the praises of their Lord. Hearing and seeing this, Christ rejoices. To such as these He gives His peace. Where there are two together there also He is present.[21]

What qualities from this quotation describe your marriage? What qualities from this quotation would you like to describe your relationship in the future?

Answers will be unique to each couple.

_____

_____

3. In 2 Timothy 4:7, Paul reflects on his life and speaks of fighting the good fight. Relate this to your marriage. What are things that you must fight, for or against, in order to maintain a healthy Christian marriage?

For quality time alone with my spouse

Against impure thoughts that lead to sin

For communication

4. To fight the fight and finish the race requires keeping the faith. Referring to Ecclesiastes 4:9–12, what are practical ways that we keep the faith in our marriage?

It is important that we all realize that we keep the faith in our marriages by keeping our faith with God first.

Nothing will help us more as a couple than for us as individuals to walk

in faith with Jesus Christ on a daily basis.

PART III. Making it personal

Complete this exercise for your own personal growth. These responses will not be shared in the group unless you want to share them.

To help you think about the goals you might want to have in your marriage, complete the following questions.

1. What do I want for me?

_____

_____

_____

2. What do I want for you?

_____

_____

_____

3. What do I want for us?

_____

_____

_____

Based on your answers and discussions choose goals you want to set for your marriage.

Long-Term Goals:

_____

_____

_____

Short-Term Goals:

_____

_____

_____

PART IV. Winding down

1. Have a side-track time. If there is time and interest, discuss whatever the group wants to talk about. You may want to have a time of sharing what the supper club has meant to each couple.

2. Talk about whether you want to continue to get together and study through Part 2 of *The Marriage Track*.

3. Plan an Ultimate Supper Club Party. Pick a date to get together.

4. Close with the following quotation and a time of prayer.

The quotation comes from Father Gabriel Calvo, the founder of Marriage Encounter, who has devoted his life to helping couples and families. It is taken from his book, *Face to Face*, and is his "Golden Rule About Marriage." In light of the fact that in God's ultimate plan, marriage is two people created and called to become one with God, he offers this:

> All that promotes genuine unity between husband and wife and between the married couple and God is in accordance with God's vision and plan.

> All that endangers, hinders, or corrupts genuine unity between husband and wife and between the married couple and God is against God's vision and plan.[22]

If you follow Father Calvo's golden rule, you're well on the way to having an ultimate growing and enriched marriage partnership!

Ultimate Marriage Builder Resources The Ultimate Supper Club

MARRIAGE RESOURCES

52 Dates for You and Your Mate—by Claudia and Dave Arp, 52 tested dates for those who want to make their marriage come alive with fun, laughter, and good times together. Nashville: Thomas Nelson Publishers, 1993.

The Marriage Track—by Claudia and Dave Arp, How to keep your relationship headed in the right direction. Nashville: Thomas Nelson Publishers, 1992.

60 One-Minute Marriage Builders—Provides sixty ways to increase intimacy and build fun into your marriage. Nashville: Thomas Nelson Publishers, 1993.

FAMILY RESOURCES

The Big Book of Family Fun, by Claudia Arp and Linda Dillow is a fun-packed resource for parents. Filled with creative, easy, and relationship-building activities for any family, this book is a must for every home. Nashville: Thomas Nelson Publishers, 1994.

Parents Encouraging Parents (PEP) Groups for MOMS video package by Claudia Arp contains a five-part video series entitled *Building Positive Relationships with Children*, a director's handbook, MOMS small group leader's guide, and individual study books. Elgin, Illinois: David C. Cook Publishing Company, 1994.

PEP for PARENTS of TEENS video package, by Dave and Claudia Arp, contains a five-part video series entitled *Building Positive Relationships for the Teen Years,* a Director's Handbook, Leader's Guide, and individual study books for participants. Elgin, Illinois: David C. Cook Publishing Company, 1994.

60 One-Minute Family Builders, and *60 One-Minute Memory Makers*, by Dave and Claudia Arp, are 2 special little books to help you use the time you do have to build your own family team. Nashville: Thomas Nelson Publishers, 1993.

52 Ways To Be a Great Mother-In-Law, by Claudia Arp, contains practical helps for keeping extended family relationships healthy. Nashville: Thomas Nelson Publishers, 1993.

WORKSHOPS BY DAVE AND CLAUDIA ARP

Marriage Alive Workshop—A fun-filled, interactive, six-hour workshop to help you fine-tune your marriage and get your marriage on track. Topics covered are High Priority Marriage, Encouragement, Finding Unity in Diversity, Communication, and Goal Setting.

PEP for Parents of Teens Workshop—Our job as parents is to work ourselves out of a job and into a relationship that will last a lifetime. The Arps share how to regroup, relate, release, and relax while parenting adolescents.

PEP for Parents Workshop—The problem with being a parent is that by the time you are qualified, you're unemployed. The Arps share key biblical insights and practical tips about parenting in the '90s and how to actually enjoy the process.

To schedule a workshop with the Arps or to find a
workshop near you, contact

MARRIAGE ALIVE INTERNATIONAL
P.O. Box 90303
Knoxville, TN 37990
(615) 691–8505

Notes

1. David and Vera Mace, "Close Companions," *Continuum* (New York: 1992), p. 45.

2. Jeanette and Robert Lauer, "Marriages Made to Last," *Marriage and Family in a Changing Society*, edited by James M. Henslin (New York: The Free Press, 1992), p. 483.

3. Adapted from Dr. Clifford and Joyce Penner, *52 Ways to Have Fun, Fantastic Sex* (Nashville: Thomas Nelson, 1994).

4. Adapted from Dave and Jeanie Stanley's workshop, *What Now, My Love?*, given at the 1993 United Marriage Encounter International Celebration.

5. Robert S. Trotter, *Marriage and Family in a Changing Society* (New York: The Free Press, 1992), pp. 145–153.

6. From David and Vera Mace, *A.C.M.E. Newsletter*, Vol. 16, No. 4, April, 1988.

7. Adapted from *Marriage Partnership Magazine*, "What's Your Minimum Daily Faith Requirement?" Summer, 1991, p. 46. Used by permission.

8. Adapted from *PEP Groups for MOMS* (Chicago: David C. Cook, 1994).

9. Adapted from David and Vera Mace, *How to Have a Happy Marriage* (Nashville: Abingdon Press, 1977), pp. 112–114.

10. Adapted from Dave and Claudia Arp, *The Marriage Track* (Nashville: Thomas Nelson, 1992).

11. Adapted from *Marriage Partnership Magazine*, "Isn't It Time Someone Took Out the Garbage?" Spring, 1993, pp. 36–37. Used with permission.

12. From A.C.M.E. Newsletter, Vol. 16, No. 3, 1988.

13. Adapted from "Making Room for Sex" by Dave and Claudia Arp, *Parents of Teenagers*, July/August, 1992, p. 21.

14. Adapted from *52 Dates for You and Your Mate* (Nashville: Thomas Nelson, 1993).

15. Adapted from *The Marriage Track* (Nashville: Thomas Nelson, 1992).

16. Adapted from *52 Ways to Have Fun, Fantastic Sex* by Dr. Clifford and Joyce Penner (Nashville: Thomas Nelson, 1994), pp. 47–49.

17. Evelyn Moschetta, "25 Ways to Make Your Marriage Sillier," *Ladies Home Journal*, May 1993, p. 92.

18. Adapted from *Marriage Partnership Magazine*, "Ever Feel Like You're Married to Your Work?" Spring, 1993, p. 24. Used with permission.

19. Adapted from *Marriage Partnership Magazine*, "Looking Ahead," Summer, 1993, pp. 59–60. Used with permission.

20. David and Vera Mace, *Men, Women and God* (Atlanta: John Knox Press, 1976), p. 15.

21. Ibid.

22. Gabriel Calvo, *Face to Face* (St. Paul: International Marriage Encounter, 1988) p. 106.

About the Authors

Dave and Claudia Arp are family life educators, marriage and family workshop leaders, and the founders of Marriage Alive International. The Arps are columnists with *Christian Parenting Today* magazine and have a daily nationally syndicated radio program, *The Family Workshop*. Together, they have authored a number of books including *The Marriage Track, 52 Dates for You and Your Mate*, and the popular *60 One-Minute Family Builder* series. The Arps are also developers of the church curriculum, PEP Groups for PARENTS. Dave and Claudia Arp are the parents of three sons and live in Knoxville, Tennessee.